Lighthouse Keepers & Coast Guard Cutters

Heroic Lighthouse Keepers And The Coast Guard Cutters Named After Them

Frederick Stonehouse

Avery Color Studios, Inc.
Gwinn, Michigan

ISBN 1-892384-03-5

Library of Congress Catalog Card Number

00-133568

First Edition 2000

Published by
Avery Color Studios, Inc.
Gwinn, Michigan 49841

Cover photograph ©William A. Britten
zuma.lib.utk.edu/lights
Cutter photo Marinette Marine Corporation

Table Of Contents

Foreword

Keepers and Cutters is a complicated book. Many themes are intertwined. There are tales of storm and shipwreck, desolation and loneliness, blinding fogs and booming cannon, lifeless bodies buried under rubble and wave, sturdy ships and blown out sails. But always, running deep and true, it is a narrative of heroic men and women who kept the lights. Some performed a single act of overwhelming courage. Others, spread their valor out over decades.

The book focuses on 14 old-time lightkeepers and what they did to inspire the Coast Guard to honor them by having an entire class of vessels, or in Coast Guard parlance, "cutters," named after them.

It is also a story of the life and times of the keepers. How they did their jobs, the daily routine, the lamps and lenses, trials and tribulations of keeping the lights burning bright.

And finally, the book is about the ships themselves, the company that designed and built them, how the Coast Guard will use them and the vessels they are replacing.

The old Lighthouse Service always named it's tenders after flowers and the new 225-foot *Juniper* class continues that great tradition. Naming the new 175-foot Keeper class tenders after people, breaks with that tradition, honoring humans rather than flowers. There are times when traditions should be broken and this is surely one of them. In the early days of the Lighthouse Service, there were no heroes and rather than pay homage to mere politicians, the Service elected to use the innocuous flower concept. But after more than two hundred years of lightkeeping, there are plenty of heroes and honoring them is an idea long over due. Three cheers for the Coast Guard for helping to keep the lights of courage and duty burning bright.

I

LIGHTHOUSES

General

To fully understand the stories of the keepers and their lighthouses, the reader must have some appreciation of the role and operation of the humble lighthouse in navigating United States waters. The following overview is an attempt to provide enough information to place the stories into an acceptable historical context; show how the lights developed and operated, the personalities and organizations integral to their success, and afford an understanding of the broad applications of the equipment and devices used.

The first lighthouse built by the colonists was established in 1716, at Little Brewster Island at the entrance to Boston Harbor. Others soon followed. Some were erected by cities, others by merchants. Providing lighthouses was not immediately perceived as a government responsibility. Following the American Revolution the control of the lights was retained by the individual states. After the 1789 constitution, lighthouses were centralized under the Treasury Department. By this time there were a dozen active beacons along the east coast.

Organization

Although the lights were initially placed under the Treasury Department in 1789, however the department was unprepared to manage them. Responsibility for the lights became a hot potato within the department, bouncing between different offices. In 1820, it was finally given to Stephen Pleasonton, the Fifth Auditor, who also assumed the title of General Superintendent of Lights. He kept the potato for 32 years. His duties included administering contracts, responding to Congressional inquires and generally overseeing the Lighthouse Service, such as it was. It was a thankless job for

Minot's Ledge Lighthouse. Author's collection.

Pleasonton. A bookkeeper by profession, he had neither the maritime nor engineering background required to administer the duties in a competent manner. In addition, the position called for a man of high intelligence, great foresight and high management ability. He possessed none of these attributes, but instead seems to have been the perfect bureaucrat. He utterly failed to realize his responsibility for the lives of ship's crews and passengers and that he owed them the best navigational aids possible. He focused only on economy and never on quality. Witnesses reported he once stated he built lighthouses cheaper than any one else and returned more money to the general fund than any other department. In all the lighthouse literature, no one has a good word to say about Stephen Pleasonton.

Local customs collectors were given the additional job of superintending the lighthouses in their districts, including their operation and construction. In consideration of the extra work, they were given a two and a half percent commission on lighthouse disbursements.

While significant growth occurred during this period, overall management was poor. The attempt was generally to spend the least possible amount of money without regard to securing acceptable equipment or results. Contracts for construction and supplies and appointing keepers were based on political affiliation, not merit. There are many instances of poor construction and lighthouse being built in the wrong place. The poor lights caused a rising chorus of complaints from sailors, ship owners and insurers.

In 1837-38, Congress investigated the lighthouse operation and made a number of recommendations for improvement. Most of them Pleasonton simply ignored. Another Congressional inquiry was held in 1842, with more recommendations following. Pleasonton ignored them too!

Finally the complaints grew so loud that in 1851, Congress directed the Secretary of the Treasury to convene a special board to investigate the situation. The board's report was thorough, concluding that the lighthouse establishment was poorly managed in both economy and efficiency. Keepers were ill-trained and in many cases incompetent and the lamps and reflectors were obsolete and inferior in design. During Pleasonton's reign the country's lighthouses were doubtless the worst in the civilized world.

Responding to the investigation, Congress in 1852, established through legislation, a nine member Lighthouse Board with the Secretary of the Treasury as ex-officio president. Other members included scientists, US Army engineers, US Navy officers and members of the US Coast Survey. The new Board organized the lights into twelve districts. Two of them were on the Great Lakes.

The Board also appointed an inspector for each district, giving him the responsibility of building and maintaining the lights and equipment as well as buying supplies. The inspector was required to inspect each station in the district once every three months. As the number of lights increased, additional help was provided for the inspector. An Army Engineer officer assisted with construction and maintenance duties. Local collectors of customs were kept on as lighthouse superintendents, having the responsibility of appointing and paying keepers and handling routine fund disbursements. Eventually their role was phased out completely.

The Board established detailed operating procedures carefully spelling out actions to be accomplished. For example, in May of every year, the following actions were required to be taken:

1. Issue proposals for supplying rations and fuel to the crews of light-vessels for the fiscal year ensuing from the first July. (See printed forms in the office.)

2. Inspect, test and receive, if of proper quality, the second lot of oil for the lights on the Atlantic coast; make out and forward bills, and remit funds for their payment.

3. Refit and dispatch supply-vessels in continuation of delivering annual supplies.

4. Issue proposals for keeping the buoys (specially authorized by the Board,) in those localities in which they cannot be attended to by the tenders, for the ensuing year.

Detailed procedures were also spelled out for the daily routine of the office processes and management of Lighthouse Service accounts.

Central depots served as stationing locations for the lighthouse tenders and for storing and forwarding supplies. Repairs to the various apparatus were also accomplished there by specially trained craftsmen such as blacksmiths, mechanics and lampists. Depots were located in each district to more efficiently support the lights.

Improvements under the Board's leadership were significant. They established lights where needed and made certain they were well kept and reliable. Inefficient men were fired. The Board also experimented with new technology, trying whatever new equipment or fuels they thought might offer improvement. Before the advent of the Board, the US provided the worst lights in the civilized world. Afterwards, we had the best. The Board also started a system of classifying lights based on the size of the lenses. The new method organized the lights into seven orders, with first order being the largest and seventh the smallest. Later the system would be changed to one based on candlepower.

Early lightkeepers often were selected based on political loyalties. Trustworthiness, reliability or competence were not requirements; political affiliation was. Congressmen with a lighthouse in their district didn't hesitate to use the appointment of a keeper as a real plum for a deserving bootlicker. Although the actual appointment of a keeper was the responsibility of the

Lightkeepers were not always the most trustworthy men. Author's collection.

local collector of customs, these worthies were relatively far down the political food chain. Depending on the results of an election, wholesale dismissals and appointments were made. This happened so frequently that in the interest of efficiency and economy, the Lighthouse Board had blank forms printed to use when it was necessary to notify keepers that they had been replaced!

Just because a keeper was of the right party and had a job didn't mean he was safe from efforts to remove him. Sometimes, "concerned citizens" would write letters to the Board complaining that the light started out the evening bright and clear, but that after a couple of hours it was extinguished. Obviously the keeper wasn't doing his job! Usually the writer offered to take his place.

The Lighthouse Board was well aware of the problem and tried it's best to minimize the deleterious effect of politics and achieved some limited success. It did establish standards for the keepers to meet, which included a three month probationary period. After being tested on his duties by the district inspector or engineer, he could be dismissed for failure.

By the late 1870's, political appointments were largely confined to the entry level positions of a third or fourth assistant keeper at the bigger lights. The keeper or first assistant were generally career positions filled by cadre personnel.

After the Civil War it was common to see veterans appointed as keepers as a reward for war service. In other instances the death of a keeper often resulted in the appointment of his wife or daughter as keeper, dependent on circumstance. The Civil War had upset the operation of the Lighthouse

Lightkeepers often became experienced small boat handlers. Author's photo.

Service since the engineers and inspectors were all military men and the war necessitated their reassignment to more pressing duties. Southern forces also captured a number of lights, destroying many of them and creating havoc for the Lighthouse Service.

The Board worked hard to get or keep good men (or women). Vacancies usually occurred only by death, resignation or dismissal. The last was invariably due to drunkenness or failure to properly keep the light. The biggest cause of keeper loss was resignation. For example, between 1885-1889, the Lighthouse Board hired 1,190 new keepers and 680, or well over half, resigned. The Board was steadfast in saying that the men were not leaving because of low pay, but more likely the result of isolation and the heavy demands of the job. Although a lightkeeper's pay was comparatively low, it was considerably more than a Life Saving Service keeper received. In cases where the two stations were located next to one another, there was often a degree of contention between the two keepers. The fact that the lifesaver, who regularly risked his life and those of his crew in the worst of storms, was paid less than the lightkeeper, who likely remained snug and safe in his nice warm lighthouse, was an unconscionable act by the government.

In spite of the disparity with the Life Saving Service, Lighthouse keepers were never well paid. The pay tended to be higher at the isolated stations and at those stations that had more work. For example if the station had a fog signal or did not have an assigned assistant. In 1857, wages were set at $400 yearly for keepers and $250 for assistants. By the 1860s wages for keepers went up to $560 and $400 for a first assistant. Determining the actual value of the wages could be difficult because of the extras the Service sometimes provided. Based on station hardships, the Service sometimes provided rations of basic staples and fuel. For example, in the mid-1880s, the principal keeper at Lake Superior's Stannard's Rock Station, considered the most isolated light in the United States, received a salary of $800 and two cords of wood.

The Lighthouse Board and later Bureau of Lighthouses, established high standards for keepers and held them to the mark. Neither organization tolerated mistakes. They investigated and if necessary took appropriate action, including dismissal. Drunkenness, sleeping on duty or being absent from the station without authorization were considered major offenses and dismissal was a common penalty.

It wasn't until 1884, that uniforms were prescribed for keepers in an attempt to create a sense of pride among the men. Female keepers however had no uniform requirement. The uniforms were intended for official or formal occasions, such as when the inspector made his, "white glove" inspection or national holidays when visitors might be expected. The first uniform was given to the keepers. Afterwards they were expected to purchase uniform replacements as needed. For a while the men wore regular clothing on normal work days. Later the uniform requirement was extended to include anytime the keeper was on duty.

The public outcry against the evils of the spoils system finally resulted in the passage by Congress in 1883, of the Pendleton Civil Service Act. Under it, appointments to key government positions would be based on ability, and special examinations were required of all applicants. Although initially only a few agencies were covered by the act, later presidents gradually increased the number. In 1896, President Cleveland added the US Lighthouse Service and from then on appointments were based on merit. Following World War I, special consideration was often given to wounded veterans, a most laudable effort on behalf of those who so bravely served.

To increase efficiency, in 1903, the Service was transferred to the new Department of Commerce and Labor. During the period of rapid growth, the old Lighthouse Board system of management became too cumbersome. It was felt the jolt of moving to the new Commerce Department might rejuvenate it. It did not. In 1910, Congress abolished the Lighthouse Board and established in its stead the Bureau of Lighthouses. The new organization remained under the Commerce Department. Instead of the nine member board, there was now only one man, the Commissioner of Lighthouses. From 1910 - 1935, the Commissioner was George R. Putnam, an experienced and energetic Coast and Geodetic Survey engineer. Under his able leadership the new organization continued to push technology to improve lighthouse efficiency. An example is the use of radio beacons which became an important element of navigation safety. By 1925, there were 13 radio fog signals in the second, third, fifth and eleventh districts (selected east coast and Great Lakes areas).

The new commissioner had the authority to organize not more than 19 districts, each to be headed by a civilian inspector. An Army Engineer officer assigned to each district continued the role of providing professional expertise to lighthouse design, construction and maintenance. The entire organization was firmly under civilian control and leadership.

The historic growth of America's lighthouses was phenomenal. In 1852, there were 331 lighthouses and 42 lightships nationwide. By 1910, there were 1,462 lighthouses and 51 lightships! In 1925, the system reached a total of 1,951 lighthouses, 46 lightships and 14,900 other navigational aids.

As in the old US Life Saving Service, a viable retirement system was slow in coming. Keepers were forced to remain in their jobs, even if old or infirm, since they had no other option. In 1916, for example, there were 92 keepers service-wide over 70 years old and 24 men with over 40 years of service. The life-savers finally got their retirement in 1915, when they merged with the US Revenue-Marine to form the Coast Guard. Three years later Congress recognized the arduous nature of the Lighthouse Service work and authorized voluntary retirement at 65 after 30 years of service and mandatory retirement at 70.

On July 7, 1939, in another move for greater governmental efficiency, President Roosevelt abolished the Bureau of Lighthouses and transferred its duties to the Coast Guard. The Coast Guard operated under the Treasury Department, so lighthouses that had started under the Treasury Department had now returned.

As part of the process of integrating into the Coast Guard, lighthouse personnel were given the option of either retaining their civilian status or converting to a military position. About half of the keepers elected to transfer into the Coast Guard. The rest stayed as civilian keepers. The integration did not go smoothly. Many Lighthouse Service men had little desire to accept military discipline or customs. In fact, the Lighthouse Service had it's own customs and traditions and were looking forward to celebrating it's sesquicentennial on August 7, 1939, when FDR's unexpected mandate was issued. A strong argument could be made that FDR's order was nothing more than pure politics. He was showing the public he was making decisions to increase theoretical government efficiency at the expense of the actual efficiency of the Service.

An example of the type of regulation the old wickies wanted to avoid is the in the February 1940, *Coast Guard Bulletin.* Circular 153, concerning Coast Guard uniforms for members of the old Lighthouse Service, established a time limit of three months for the men to obtain them. It allowed an exception for those officers who would reach the statutory retirement age of 64 before January 1, 1945. It was optional for these men to obtain the, "...frock coat, evening dress coat, boat cloak, white evening dress trousers, cocked hat, epaulettes, full dress belt, and black patent-leather shoes."[1] Can you picture a lighthouse keeper so adorned? The seagulls would die laughing!

Construction

To withstand the ravages of storms, the lights were well constructed of brick or stone. Wood may have been used for mere range lights, but never for, "real" lights. They tended to be square in shape and plain in design with no emphasis placed on anything, "frivolous." The lights were not usually "one of a kind," but built from standard plans and designs. For example, on Lake Superior, Au Sable light, eight miles east of Grand Marais, Michigan and the Outer Island Light in the Apostle Islands, Wisconsin, were both built in 1874,

Range Light at Presque Isle, Lake Huron, Michigan. An exception to the rule, range lights were often built of wood. Brandon Stonehouse photo.

from the same plans. Big Bay Point and Fourteen Mile Point lights, also both on Lake Superior, were also near twins. In many instances however, the basic design was modified to meet a particular site requirement.

Usually the light station would consist of a compound of several buildings: the lighthouse proper, a combination tower and dwelling, an oil house and a fog signal house. A pier or dock was also built to facilitate the landing of personnel and supplies. Boat houses and other out buildings were usually later additions to the compound.

Generally there were two lighthouse types, off shore towers and land lights. The off shore towers were directly exposed to the sea. *Off shore towers* were built four different ways. Masonry towers were constructed of cement, concrete or stone and were circular in shape, allowing little purchase for the waves regardless of how they struck the structure. The towers were anchored

The stone tower of the lighthouse at Lake Huron's Spectacle Reef was built to withstand not only the ravages of wind and wave, but also the power of the ice. Author's collection.

Some lights were built strictly as harbor entrance beacons, as that at Oswego, New York. U.S. Coast Guard photo.

firmly to a rock base, above or below the water. *Steel or iron towers* were built when there was no good natural anchorage such as rocks would provide. Metal piles were driven or screwed into the bottom to keep the towers in place. *Cast iron towers* were made of iron instead of masonry materials but otherwise were very similar. *Caisson towers* were built on soft bottoms by sinking the foundations until they rested on a firm base.

Lightships

A number of lightships were also used in the areas were vessel courses ran close to dangerous reefs or shoals and it was impractical to erect a permanent lighthouse. In some instances, lightships were used until permanent stations were built.

The first lightship, the *Nore*, was established in England in 1732, at the mouth of the Thames while the first in the U.S. was stationed on the Chesapeake Bay near Norfolk, Virginia in 1820.

The classic lightship was built high in the bow and of heavy overall construction. The ship was designed to stay in position and to kill if

Lansing Shoal *Lightship. Note the daymarks on the masts and lowered lanterns. U.S. Coast Guard photo.*

A lightship's greatest fear! Author's collection.

necessary. There is always the danger of collision. Should such a disaster occur, it is the lightship that will usually survive. The loss of the merchant vessel is bad enough, but the loss of the lightship provided the opportunity for other ships to blunder into the reef without the lightship there to warn them off. It is better to have one ship wrecked than many. Therefore, the lightship was made strong! There were 150 instances nationwide, of major collisions between lightships and other vessels. Only five resulted in the loss of the lightship, a ratio that speaks volumes about the strength of these little ships!

One lightship that didn't survive collision was Lightship No. 117. In May 1934, she was anchored on station off Nantucket Island when she was run down by the big passenger liner SS *Olympic* (the sister ship of the *Titanic*). All of the lightship crew were saved. Subsequent investigation showed the *Olympic* was "riding the beam," steering directly down the lightship's radio direction finder signal until the foghorn was heard, when she was to turn clear. It was a very dangerous practice. In this instance, the horn was not heard in time and the steamer cut the little lightship in two!

The number of lightships in service peaked in 1909, when 56 were employed in American waters. Besides the lightships on station, there were a number of relief ships prepared to replace the regular ships for maintenance or accident.

CLEANING THE LAMPS.

Crew cleaning a lightship's lenses. Author's collection.

Fog was always dreaded by the lightship crews, not only because of the inherent visibility problems and increased chance of collision, but also because the whistle or bell had to be sounded. The mournful blasts added immeasurably to the general feeling of depression for the crews. The longer the fog lasted, the greater the depression.

Lightkeeping on a lightship was much worse than that ashore or on a tower station. On the beach a man had a chance to take a walk, visit a friend, or receive company. Isolation was not normally a terrible problem. On fixed towers such as Stannard's Rock or Spectacle Reef, long walks were out of the

HOT COFFEE.

A lightship mess room. Note the "raised edges" of the table to keep the dinnerware from smashing to the floor in a seaway. The stove is also heavily secured. Author's collection.

question and isolation a constant companion. At least ashore or on a tower, the damn things didn't move. A man could put his feet down firmly on rock or stone and not be required to hold on for dear life. Lightships were rarely still, whether the weather was fair or foul. The most experienced sailors often suffered from appalling bouts of seasickness from the unique motion of the lightships. One lightship keeper remarked, "If it weren't for the disgrace it would bring my family, I'd rather go to the state's prison."

Lamps, Lenses and Lights

The basic essential for a navigation light of course was flame to provide an illumination source. A bonfire on a hill could fill this role, but was far from efficient and it's visibility was very limited. When towers were built, the fire was transferred to the top, increasing efficiency only marginally. Coal later replaced wood since it burned longer and brighter. An open coal fire had a range of eight to ten miles during normal weather. During periods of low cloud, the glow could actually be reflected a greater distance. In stormy weather however, such fires could not be seen from the weather side where they were most needed. When reflectors and glass chimneys were introduced, the soot soon degraded them. Candles were also tried but their illumination was weak. Later "spider lamps" were used. Essentially they were only a pan of oil with four wicks extending from the corners. Boston Light used them in 1790, and in some areas they remained in use until 1812. A significant

Built during the Roman period, circa 50 AD, Pharos Light in Dover, UK, was an important early aid to navigation in the English Channel. Author's photo.

problem of the lamp was the very acrid fumes they gave off, limiting the amount of time a keeper could work in the lamp room. The introduction of the Argand lamp in 1871, was a major advancement. Argand lamps were developed by Aimee Argand of Geneva, Switzerland and used a burner with a hollow wick in a glass chimney.

The first major improvement in U.S. lights came about through the efforts of Captain Winslow Lewis. Born in Wellfleet, Massachusetts in 1770, he was a successful sea captain until 1807, when an economic down turn forced him to leave the sea and seek his fortune ashore. Although he had little formal

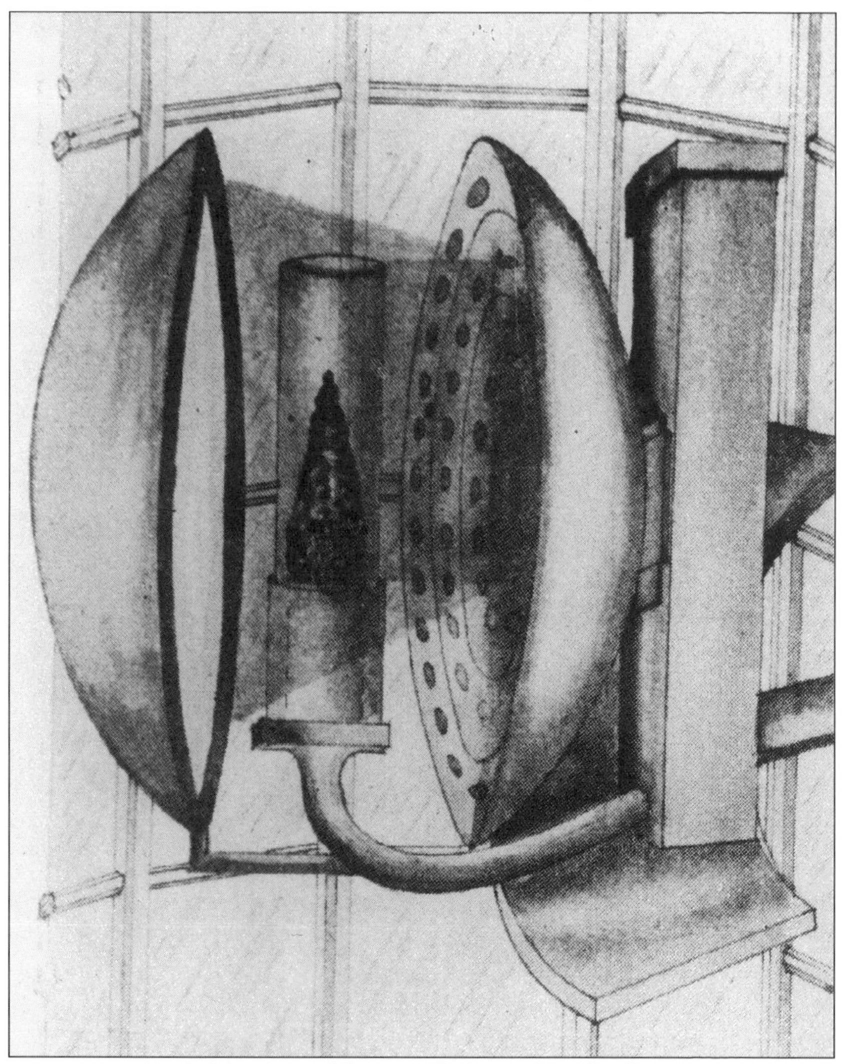

A primitive Argand lamp. U.S. Coast Guard collection.

education, he believed he could improve the nation's lights. In June 1810, he patented a device later to be known as the "Lewis" lamp. It was the first "standard" U.S. lamp. About 1812, Winslow Lewis convinced his good friend Stephen Pleasonton, the infamous "Fifth Auditor," to buy a lamp he designed and patented based on those currently in use in Europe. This was all rather strange since Lewis once confessed he knew nothing about lighthouse optics! He called his device a, "magnifying and reflecting lantern," for lighthouse work, which he claimed was a combined reflector, lamp and magnifier. Later experts called it, "...as crude a device as ever emanated from the brain of an inventive man." [2] The reflectors were made of thin copper plate with a scanty silver coating. The lens, called a magnifier by Lewis, was a circular piece of green bottle glass two and a half by four inches in diameter. One inspector said it only, "...made a bad light worse." Another testified that it was, "...worse than useless." Lewis did not argue against the criticism, but did point out the great savings in oil his device provided, using roughly half of that of the European lamps. He had also structured his contract such that instead of money, he was paid in oil, receiving one-half of the oil his device saved. After the first five years of his contract, his devices had saved so much oil that the terms were modified by the government to one-third of the oil saved since the government believed it was far too lucrative for Lewis! In it's basic form Winslow's device used an Argand lamp inside of a parabolic reflector with the addition of a solid piece of glass as a crude lens. To increase the power of the light and it's horizontal visibility, a number of lamps, each with it's own reflector, were mounted together in a configuration called a chandelier. A series of rings, adjustment screws and other devices were used to hold the reflectors and lamps in the correct position. It was not uncommon to find 14 or more lamps in such an unwieldy arrangement, for example, each tower in the Matinicus Rock twin towers had fourteen lamps, each with a separate reflector! The Lewis devices were complicated, inefficient and difficult to maintain. The parabolic reflectors were cheaply made and often not true to form. After short use they were generally found to be bent and out of shape. The silvered reflective surface in practice was scrubbed off in a matter of months because the issued cleanser was too abrasive. The lens itself attracted smoke, in turn dimming the light even more.

Lewis was given a contract to install his devices in the 49 lighthouses then in use and to keep them in good repair for a period of four years. The government also purchased the rights to the "Lewis Lamp." He later was contracted to visit each lighthouse in person and maintain the lamps and report on the condition of the lighthouse. He was in effect, the first superintendent of lighthouses.

In 1818, he contracted to construct a lighthouse on Franks Island in the northeast pass of the Mississippi River. Lewis claimed the plans he was given by the government were unsafe and that the foundation would fail. Three days before the lighthouse was finished, the foundation collapsed, proving his evaluation correct! Lewis eventually submitted his own plans and received the contract to rebuild the light, a task he finished to satisfaction.

It is said Pleasonton frequently had his friend look at bid proposals from other contractors for his comments. Lewis often claimed that the bid prices were too high and he eventually ended up with the contract. Lewis built so many lighthouses, he drew up a set of five basic plans, on the theory that regardless of circumstances, one of his standard plans would meet the requirement.

Lewis' power over Pleasonton was such that in 1835, he abruptly changed the characteristics of the Mobile Point Lighthouse strictly on his own accord! Such a major change is only done after deep consultation with government authorities and mariners and then only after a long period of public notice. After strong complaints from mariners, Pleasonton was forced to admonish his friend.

Surprisingly one of Lewis's harshest critics was his nephew, Isaiah William Penn Lewis, usually cited as I.W.P. Lewis. He was a sailing master who later trained in civil engineering. For a while he worked for his uncle in the construction of lighthouses. Eventually he went out on his own, bidding against his uncle. One source says he obtained several contracts but bid too low. When he tried to have Pleasonton adjust the contracts, the fifth auditor refused. As he interpreted this as his uncle trying to "get him," he became a strong advocate against his uncle. In 1842, he claimed his uncle's device was copied from an English lighthouse and his reflectors were bad and lighthouses poorly built. His attacks were sharp and personal.

Winslow Lewis died on May 20, 1850. It is well he went when he did, missing the embarrassment of the change over to the Lighthouse Board and general denigration of his devices and the exposure of his cozy relationship with Pleasonton.

The first Fresnel lens in the United States was installed at Navesink Light in 1853. While only five stations were equipped with them, they had been standard in Europe for over 15 years! This lens has a powerful central lamp surrounded by refracting prisms and glass rings. The rings and prisms bend and guide the light, aiming it outward in powerful beams. In the old parabolic Lewis system, one half of the light was lost. In the Fresnel system the loss was less than ten percent, resulting in an increase of over 400 percent intensity! The Fresnel lenses were very heavy and were mounted on large iron

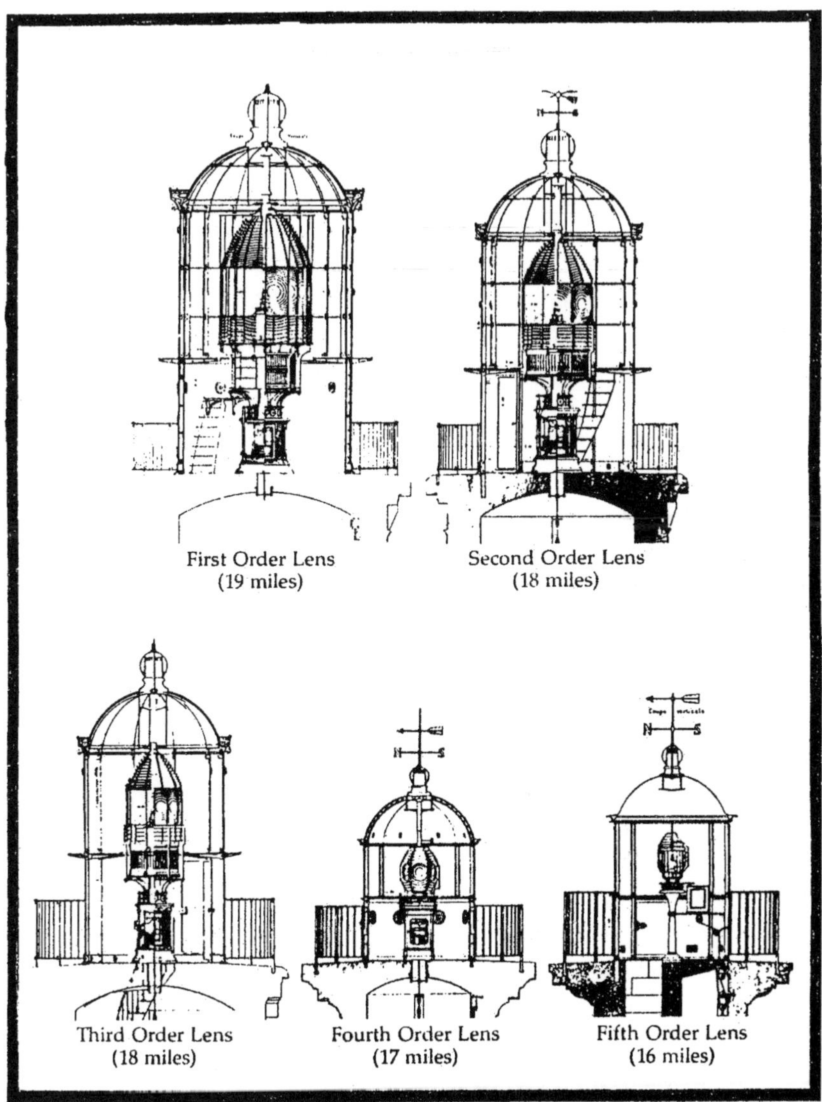

Five "orders" of Fresnel lenses. Author's collection.

pedestals. Weighing nearly three tons, a massive first order Fresnel lens had over 1,000 prisms. When it was necessary to revolve the light the lens was mounted on rollers or after 1890, floated in a trough filled with mercury if the lens was heavy enough to require it. They were so well balanced, a three ton lens could be rotated by the touch of a finger! There are cases where through accident the mercury was lost and the keepers had to make a hurried trip to the local druggist to buy a replacement supply. Handling the mercury and breathing the fumes often caused significant health problems which went unrecognized at the time. Invented in 1820, the lens was named for Augustin Fresnel, a French scientist. Throughout it's long use as a lighthouse appliance, the Fresnel lens was constantly improved in design and performance. Without question, it was the premier lighthouse lens ever developed.

Born in the French village of Broglie, Augustin was initially thought by his teachers to be "slow." As he advanced in schooling however, he exhibited an excellent ability in mathematics. At age 16 he entered the prestigious Ecole Polytechnic. This was during the reign of Napoleon and the best students were trained as military engineers. The rest, including the sickly Augustin, became civil engineers. Augustin would spend the bulk of his career building minor roads and bridges. An inquisitive mind however is tough to relegate to the boring hinterlands of France, and Augustin began to explore the theory of light. The prevailing one had been developed by Newton a century before, and was badly outdated.

The current lighthouse reflector and lens was known as a catoptric. Its' drawback was that light escaped at both the top and bottom of the device. An improvement was the dioptric or reflective lens which directed light to a desired point. Augustin's genius was to develop a lens known as a catadioptric which combined both systems. His theories of light and resulting improvements, were little accepted in his own time. In 1826, however, he was assigned as the temporary secretary to the commissioner of lighthouses. His lens were installed in several lighthouses and were so much of an improvement, they were soon installed throughout Europe. Fresnel died in 1827, at the age of 39.

Pleasonton was absolutely against the revolutionary lens and only tested it when forced to do so by Congress. Even when it proved wildly successful he refused it's purchase. It was only with the removal of the infamous Fifth Auditor that the lens was accepted into service.

Pleasonton and Lewis's role in preventing the adoption of the Fresnel lens is near criminal. Pleasonton was aware of the lens as early as 1830, but even in the face of Congressional pressure to adopt the lens, stood-by his old friend Lewis's contraption. Should the Fresnel be adopted, Lewis's lucrative business of providing his devices, would be finished. The safety of the mariner, his passengers and vessel be damned! This is business! Both men did their best to prevent lighthouse development in the U.S.

In a letter to Congressman Kennedy, Chairman of the Committee on Commerce, reporting on the original Navesink installation in 1841, Pleasonton stated, "...the cost of a lantern made under his direction (the lens

A massive first order Fresnel lens. U.S. Coast Guard photo.

company) amounting to nearly thrice as much as one can now be made for... The cost of these lenses, however is nothing compared to the beauty and excellence of the light they afford. They appear the perfection of apparatus

Fresnel lens came in seven sizes or "orders." U.S. Coast Guard photo.

for light-house purposes, having in view only the superiority of the light... There are drawbacks however, in relation to their management, which would render them unfit for use in the United States upon a large scale, there being but one lamp which supplies all the light, with three or four concentric wicks, and this lamp, made upon the carcel principal, is very apt to get out of order, and the light become extinguished, if the keeper be not an intelligent mechanic and capable of making the necessary repairs... There is not a single keeper out of about two hundred and forty, in charge of the reflector lights, so far as my knowledge extends, who is capable of taking charge of and conducting a lens light properly." [3]

Fresnel lenses were classified into seven sizes or orders, relating to their power. A sixth order lens was less than a foot in diameter. The largest lens, a first order, measured six feet in diameter and stood nearly twelve feet high. The lenses were also very expensive, a factor that discouraged their early adoption by the penny-pinching Pleasonton. Eventually, the United States shifted to the Fresnel system and realized that as a result of their efficiency in reducing fuel costs, using only a quarter of previous requirements, they soon paid for themselves. The fuel savings resulted from usually needing only one lamp burning for illumination as opposed to the many required by the Lewis system. Many of these wonderful lenses are now in museums where the public can view and appreciate the magnificent workmanship. Others were destroyed by vandals or official neglect when the lighthouses were abandoned by the government.

One of the problems with Fresnel lens was the high quality optical glass needed to make the lenses. In the early days, only two companies in France were able to produce it. In 1850, a British firm, Chance Brothers, began to manufacture it and became the only producer outside of France during this period.

The order of a light depends on the distance from the center of the light to the inner surface of the lens. This is also called the focal length. For example, a first-order lens has a focal length of thirty-six inches, or six feet total inside diameter and a third order lens twenty inches of focal length or forty inches diameter.

Many different lamps were used in the U.S. Most common however were the Carcel, Lepaute and Funck. Of the three, Funck is perhaps the most well

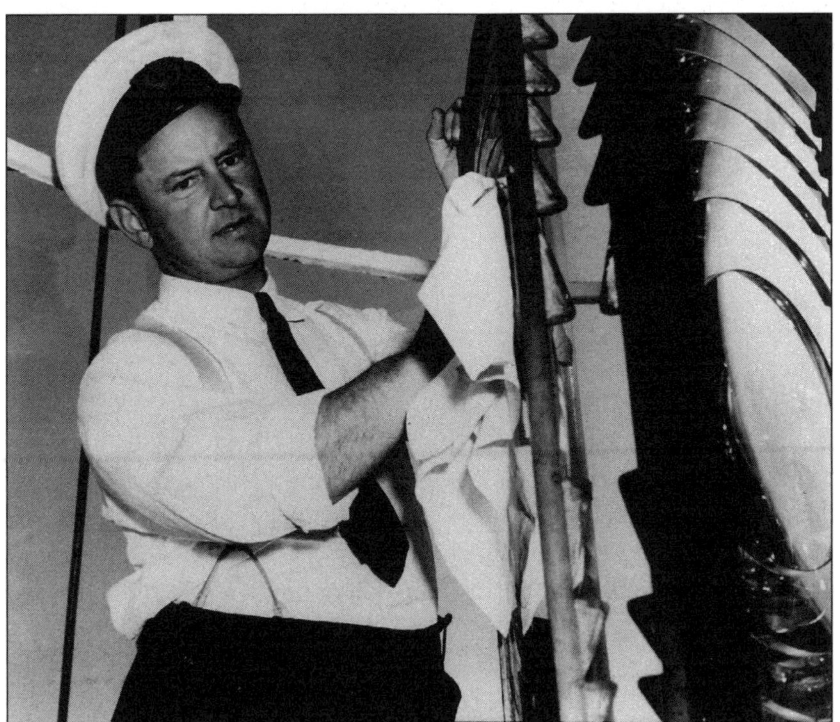

Polishing the lens was a constant job for a keeper. U.S. Coast Guard photo.

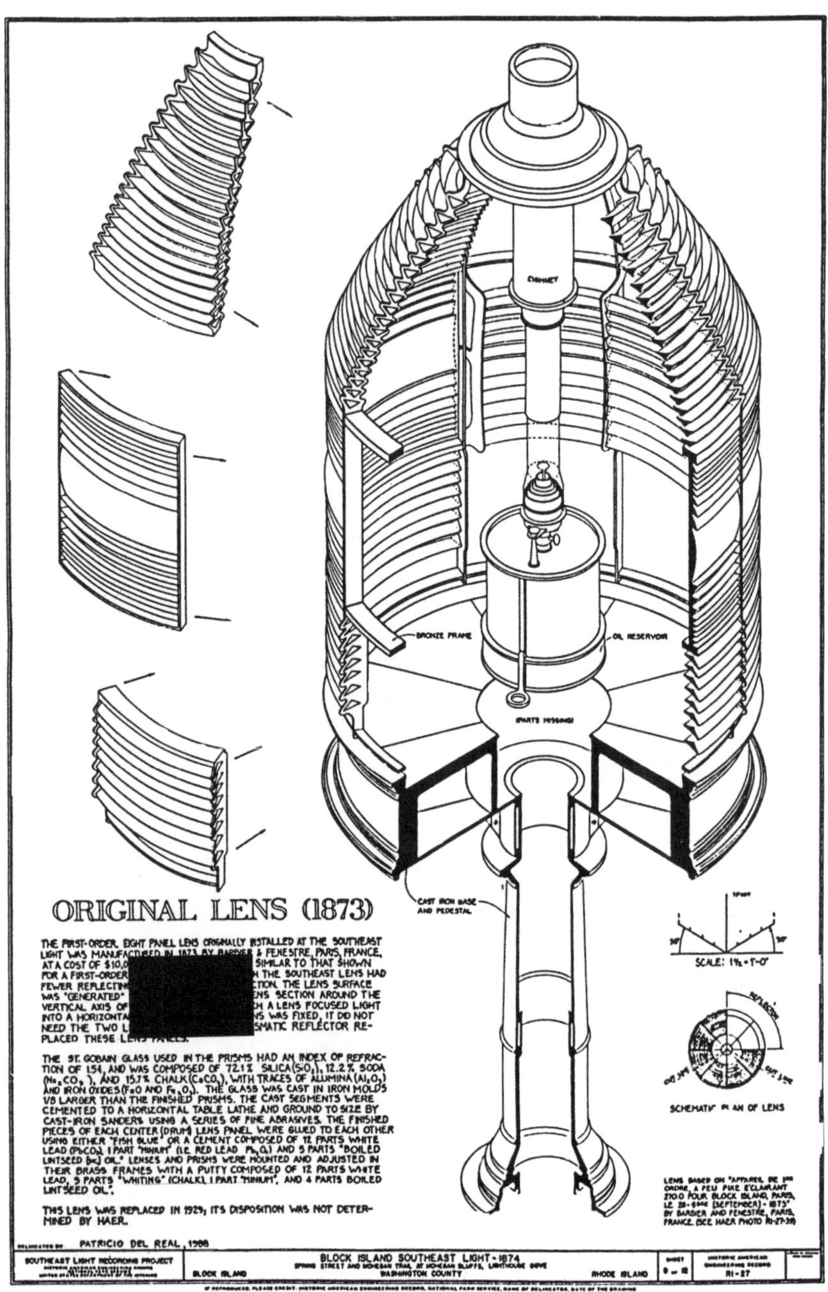

This sketch shows the basic design of a Fresnel lens. U.S. Coast Guard collection.

known, which considering he was a Lighthouse Service employee, isn't surprising. Lepaute was also a major manufacturer of Fresnel lens.

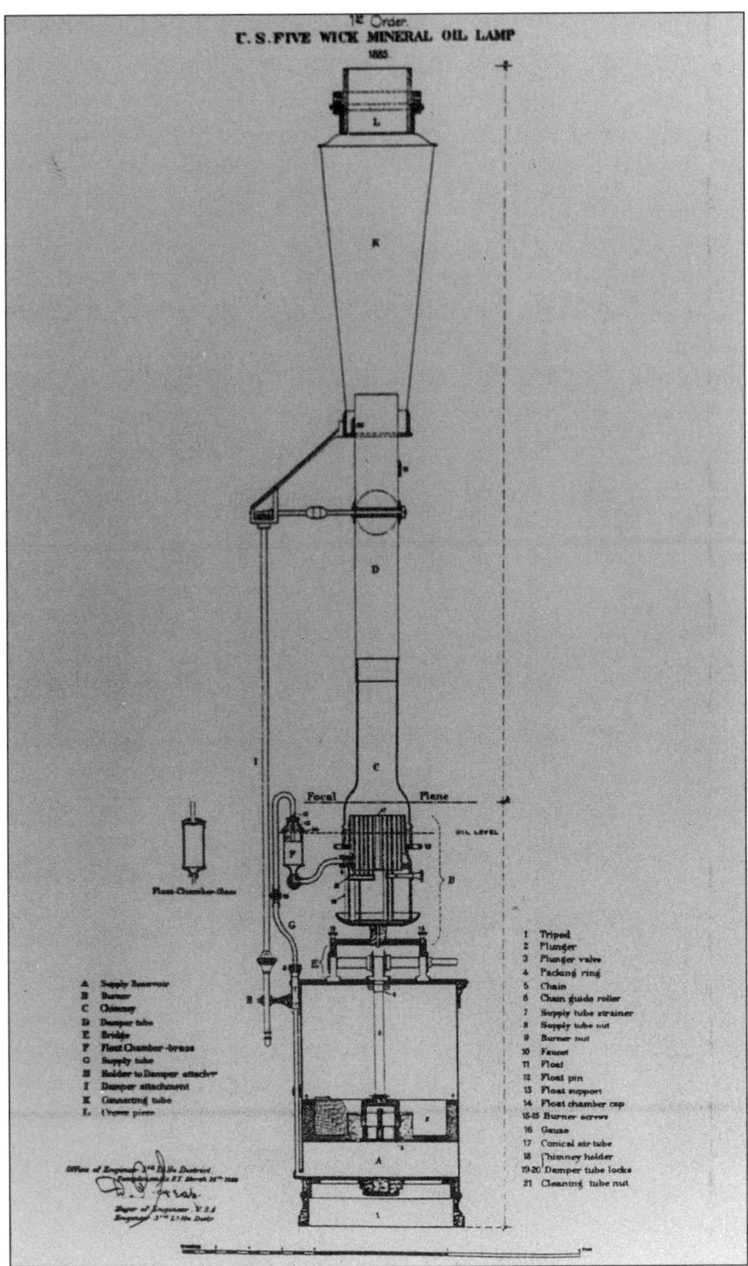

A "typical" mineral oil lamp. U.S. Coast Guard collection.

Today Fresnel lens are no longer used in lighthouses. Glass fibre reinforced plastics as a lens material was introduced in the early 1960s.

Since the new efficient lights generated low heat, lenses could now be made from plastics such as acrylic and polycarbonate.

U.S. lights, as well as all others, burned sperm whale oil until about 1864. Two varieties were used, a thicker viscosity called, "summer oil" and a thinner variant for winter use. In colder environments like Lake Superior, the oil had to be preheated before use to assure an even flow.

Today we tend to look on the use of whale oil as some sort of strange aberration from such a wondrous and majestic animal. "How could men kill such a magnificent creature just for something as mundane as oil?" What we forget is that it was whale oil that helped fuel the great industrial revolution, freeing families from slavery to the soil and allowing the galaxy of products that eventually gave us our technological society of today. On a very mundane basis, it was whale oil burning brightly and cleanly in a lonely little lighthouse that kept a ship off the deadly reef and saved all aboard. Sperm whale oil was used because simply stated, it was the best product available!

Having to warm the oil before use was often a problem, especially for a light located far out on the end of a long break water. The keeper had to carefully heat the oil ashore, then make his precarious way through storm and icy wind over a shaky wood walk way out to the light tower. Hopefully, by the time he arrived, the oil had not congealed too much for use. When the price of whale oil increased to a level the government thought too high, the fuel was switched initially to lard oil and later to kerosene or as it was then called, mineral oil.

The use of whale oil for lighthouses became a victim of the Civil War. The Confederate commerce raiders like the infamous *Shenandoah* and *Alabama* alone destroyed 46 New England whalers. Counting other loses, by the time the war ended fully half of the New England fleet was annihilated. As the result, whale oil prices dramatically increased.

For a long time kerosene was thought to be too dangerous for lighthouse use. For example, in 1864, a Lake Michigan keeper used a kerosene lamp in his light without official approval to test it's effectiveness. For several nights it apparently worked very well, it's brilliance increasing the visibility of his light markedly. The next night it exploded, throwing oil on the keeper. A second explosion blew the lantern off the tower and shattered the lens. Eventually the problems with the volatile fuel were solved and it proved highly successful. The fuel was burned through cylindrical lamp wicks, allowing for a central flow of air for improved and cleaner combustion. Arrangements of from one to five lamps were needed to provide the necessary candlepower for a given lens. By 1886, all lamps were converted to kerosene. The amount of kerosene burned was prodigious. In 1916, over

600,000 gallons of kerosene were used in the country, more than half by the Lighthouse Service.

The ultimate improvement was made in 1904, when the service changed to the use of incandescent oil vapor (I.O.V.) lamps. Operating much like a Coleman lantern, fuel is forced into a vaporizer chamber and then into a mantle. This arrangement increased brilliance many times over the old-fashioned wicks and burned far less fuel. I.O.V. was first used at the North Hook Beacon, at Sandy Hook, New Jersey.

The illuminating power from a given quantity of oil was sometimes increased by a factor of eight. I.O.V. lamps used about three-fourths gallon of kerosene a year for each candle-power of the bare lamp, as opposed to six gallons a year per lamp for the Argand lamp. When I.O.V. was introduced at Cape Hatteras the power of the light increased from 27,000 to 80,000 candle-power and the oil consumption decreased from 2280 gallons to 1300 gallons yearly.

Oil, regardless of type, was a very carefully controlled item. It was easily pilferable as it could be burned in common lanterns, either by the keeper or sold by him to others. Today we could think of this in terms of having the keys to a government gas pump in your back yard. It could be very tempting to take just, "a little" for use in the family car. Keepers were required to periodically measure the amount of oil used and record it in the logbook. Comparison with previous year records was another check for accountability. Inaccurate records, or tampering with them, resulted in reprimand, suspension of pay or dismissal. Being bedridden with illness was not considered a reasonable excuse for not keeping proper records.

When acetylene was developed in the 1920's, it largely spelled the end for the old time lightkeepers. The flow of gas for an acetylene lamp could be regulated by a, "sun-valve" that would turn the light on and off as needed. No longer would the tower stairs echo to the tread of the old wickies' footfalls at dust and dawn. Electricity was adopted as the illuminate at Dungeness Light in Britain in 1862, but was later abandoned as unreliable. U.S. lighthouse engineers used electric lights in the Statue of Liberty in 1886, and later at Navesink Lighthouse in New Jersey in 1898. Officials however believed that electric lights lacked reliability in most locations. As time passed however, both reliability and technology improved to the point that electricity eventually replaced all other illuminants

Fog Signals

Fog signals were also maintained at many lights. At first they were only hand rung bells, but by 1851, mechanically operated systems were in use.

Bells were once a popular method of signaling in fog. U.S. Coast Guard collection.

Fog horn building at Montauk Point, New York. U.S. Coast Guard photo.

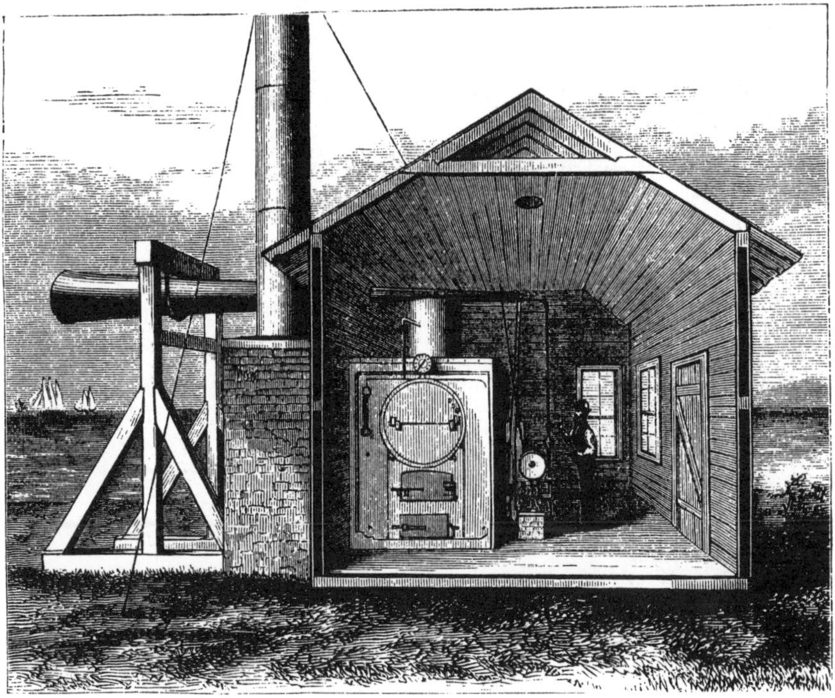

The interior of a steam generated fog signal. Note the large boiler. U.S. Coast Guard collection.

Hand operated rotary fog horn. Brandon Stonehouse photo.

Later steam whistles and sirens were adopted. Cannons were used in some stations. By 1900, nearly all fog signals were of the steam powered variety. One problem with the steam whistle, however, was the long time needed to raise the necessary steam pressure before the signal could sound. Often the process of starting a boiler fire and waiting patiently for the steam pressure to rise to a sufficient level could take as long as 45 minutes. In a busy shipping channel this was a very long time indeed. Eventually steam signals were replaced with ones using compressed air that greatly decreased response time. The compressed air was provided by gasoline or diesel engines driving special air compressors and was stored in large tanks for instant use. Regardless of the type of signal, fog still could distort sound. In some instances, a fog signal can clearly be heard five miles from the station; lost at three miles and again heard at one mile.

Flashing Lights

Developing a mechanism to make a light flash or occult, thus emitting a distinctive signal as opposed to a simple white glow, was a critical improvement to avoid confusion between lights. There were two general methods used; either to rotate the lamp and lens so that the beam was emitted only at preset intervals, or to rotate blinders around the lens. Power for either system came from a system of ropes or cables and weights wound to the top of the tower and allowed to slowly descend actuating a set of governing gears. Every so often, usually every three or four hours, the keepers had to crank the weight back up to begin the cycle again. The interval depended on the speed of rotation. In some instances, colored lights, flashing or constant, were used to differentiate lights. The lens either rotated on small wheels or "floated" on a bed of mercury.

There were three general characteristics by all lights, although there were also many various combinations of these characteristics. A *fixed light* gave a continuous light. Because they could easily be confused with lights on the shore, all of the early fixed lights were eventually converted to other characteristics. A *flashing light* showed it's beam less than the darkness, perhaps five seconds of light followed by 25 seconds of darkness. An *occulting light* showed longer than the darkness, fifteen seconds of light followed by ten seconds of darkness.

There is a 1797 reference for ordering "eclipses" from Europe for the Cape Cod Light in Massachusetts. Boston Light was fitted was a revolving light in 1811, as were several others about the same time.

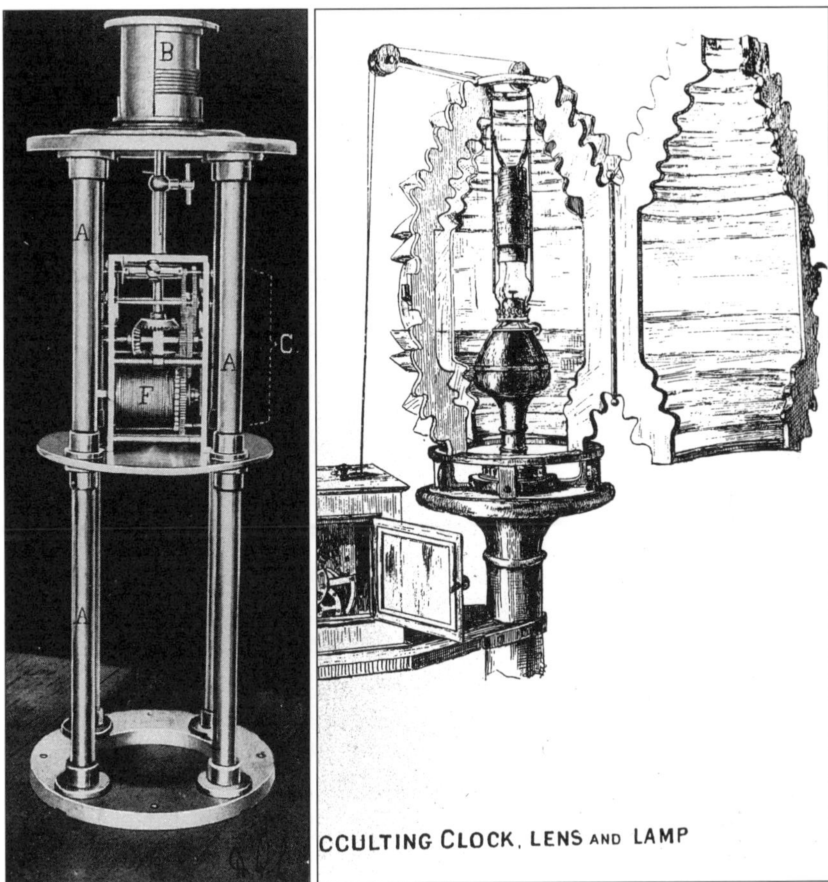

Left: a rotating mechanism for a fourth order Fresnel. U.S. Coast Guard photo. Right: a system for "occulting" a lamp. U.S. Coast Guard collection.

Submarine Signals

Early Swiss experiments in 1841, showed that sound could be transmitted through water for more than 21 miles. The first use of this new technology was in 1904. Submerged bells were placed with light ships and struck with special clappers operated by pneumatic or electrical devices. Some were also fitted to special buoys.

Radio Beacons

It is believed the first radio beacons were installed in 1921, on the U.S. lightship *Ambrose* and two stations on the shore approach. Before World War II chains of radio beacons were installed covering all of the major sea lanes.

Using the stations, each transmitting a different identification signal in Morse code, a ship could obtain it's position by taking a bearing on the signals from two or more stations.

Daily Routine

Running a light took a special kind of person. The daily routine could be difficult and was always demanding. It also was tedious and boring, depending on one's propensity for routine and repetitive work. The light had to be maintained in a constant state of readiness. The exact details of the keeper's responsibilities could be found in the publication *Instructions to Light-Keepers* provided by the Lighthouse Board. Virtually everything he needed to know was explained in laborious precision and detail. The main job of the keeper was to keep the lamp burning from sunset to sunrise. To this end, *Instructions...* gave the keeper the daily responsibilities to clean and polish the lens, check and fill the oil lamp, dust the framework of the apparatus, trim the wicks and in general assure the light was ready in all regards for the next night. It is from the work of trimming the wick that the old keepers received the nick-name, "Wickies." Every two months he was to wash the lens with alcohol and once a year polish it with a special provided rouge. The lamps were changed every 15 days. The assistant keeper, if there was one, was tasked to clean the copper and brass fixtures of the apparatus and all tools in the lantern room as well as the walls, floors and balconies. He was to sweep the tower stairs, landing, doors, windows, recesses and passageways from the lantern to oil room. At some lights he also had to shovel the piles of dead birds off the galley deck every morning. Attracted by the bright beams, the birds were killed by the dozens when they crashed into the windows. Of course if there was no assistant at the light, the keeper had to do everything. The birds hitting the light could be a real godsend. During the 1890s, a keeper at Boon Island, off the Maine coast, was wondering what to have for Thanksgiving. The day was fast approaching and none of the men were able to make it ashore for supplies. The man was standing just inside the lamproom on the day before Thanksgiving when he heard a series of heavy "thumps." Looking out on the galley, he saw a pair of ducks. Searching below the light, he found four more. The keepers certainly had a fine Thanksgiving!

When working in the lantern room, both men were required to wear linen aprons to prevent any chance of their coarse clothing scratching the valuable lens. Regulations called for the light to be ready for the night's use not later than 10:00 a.m. The grounds also had to be kept clean and orderly as well as all buildings and facilities. Station maintenance, including painting the tower, consumed the bulk of the men's time.

Painting the lighthouse tower was always an arduous task. This photo is of the tower at St. Martin Island, Lake Michigan. Bouchan Collection.

Towers were painted every spring. Usually white wash was used since it allowed the tower to "breath." Female keepers were excused from having to paint the tower or cap. Since tower height could run upward of 100 feet or more, painting or white washing was always an exciting time. Two keepers were always needed to do the job. One worked applying the fluid, while the other tended to hoisting or lowering the stage. Under normal conditions, the job could be done in six to eight hours as long as the weather cooperated. Painting the black cap on top of the lens room was even more dangerous. First a rope was thrown over the top of the dome from the galley rail and brought around to make a loop held fast by the ball and lightning rod. On the ground below, wives and children watched fearfully as a keeper hung from the rope to apply the black paint.

On the sea coast, lights were kept burning the year around while those on the Great Lakes were exhibited only during the navigation season when the lakes were ice free. Usually they were closed sometime in December and not reopened until mid-March or later. The exact dates depended on the opening of shipping. In some locations on Lake Michigan they were kept burning all year, but this is an anomaly.

Before *Instructions...* any training the keeper received was at best haphazard. The superintendent, (in reality the collector of customs) was supposed to instruct the new keeper in his duties, but this was not always done and was usually very rudimentary at best. If the new keeper was very lucky, the old one gave him detailed instructions before leaving. Usually this didn't happen. There was a written set of instructions that was supposed to be posted at each light, but an 1851 investigation discovered more of the stations without it than with it. This lack of adequate training and reference instructions can partially explain the disastrous condition of the lights before the era of the Lighthouse Board.

To help provide fresh vegetables, keepers often kept small gardens. In many instances they were not very successful since the lights were frequently located in areas that did not have good soil. In some instances keepers brought boxes of their own garden soil with them. For many years this was the practice of the keeper at Stannard's Rock Light. Located 44 miles out in Lake Superior, almost directly north of Marquette, Michigan, the light is often lashed by thundering storms. As a result the keeper constantly, "lost" his gardens to the grasping waves. Raising chickens was also popular at many lighthouses, but there could be problems. At one station the fog horn blew so loudly the chickens refused to lay eggs. At another station, a big wind came and just blew the chickens away, coop and all. At least the cow stayed on the ground!

The Lighthouse Service also provided special portable libraries. Packed into sets of roughly 50 books, the library boxes could easily be exchanged between stations. As an added bonus, the boxes were designed to stack into neat book shelves, thus helping to minimize furniture requirements. Other

The lighthouse tender Marigold *was typical of the small ships that kept the scattered lighthouses supplied. U.S. Coast Guard photo.*

keepers occupied their spare time building model boats, hunting, fishing, canning, taxidermy, agate picking or mulling through correspondence courses.

The lights were supplied by special vessels called lighthouse tenders. The first tender of the Lighthouse Service was a sailing vessel, the former Revenue Cutter *Rush*, obtained in 1840. The first government owned tender on the lakes was the schooner *Belle*, purchased in 1863, for use in the Eleventh District. Previously the work was done by contract vessels. Other famous Great Lakes tenders used at various times were *Dahlia*, *Haze*, *Crocus*, *Hyacinth*, *Warrington*, *Marigold*, *Lotus*, *Amaranth*, *Clover* and *Aspen*. On the sea coasts, the *Iris*, *Juniper*, *Mignonette*, *Mayflower*, *Maple*, *Mangrove*, *America* and *Fir* were among many tenders. Work on a tender could be dangerous. The *Mignonette* was lost in an 1887 hurricane when she was swept from her mooring in Texas. Neither ship or crew were ever heard from again.

These tough little vessels carried not only all the operating stores needed by the lights, but also the dreaded inspector. These men were infamous for their, "white glove" examinations of stations. A poor inspection could spell the end of a keeper's career.

Before the advent of the Lighthouse Board and it's system of depots and tenders, the entire chain of lighthouses were virtually administered, at least in the field by contract. Pleasonton issued a series of five year contracts for all supplies needed by the whole Service, as well as complete maintenance of all apparatus. The contractor was to visit each light once a year and provide Pleasonton with a written report of it's condition and an evaluation of the ability of the keeper. Subletting, a keeper hiring another man to actually "keep" the light, was common, further denigrating the effective execution of the requirements.

Some men handled the deadly daily routine of lightkeeping well. Others however, after a careful reading of their daily logs, appeared to, "lose their marbles." The inescapable monotony, sameness of days, weeks, months and years, and the duties that never changed, all worked at the keeper's psyche. More than one keeper was driven over the edge of sanity by the terrible grinding isolation and lack of human contact.

Not all lighthouses were lonely, desolate places. The Navesink Light in New Jersey is a fine example of an urban lighthouse. Shopping streets are within several hundred feet, as are schools, churches and the full social life of a busy community.

It is important to remember that lighthouses were built to fill a specific need in a location of known danger. The hazard could be in a lonely and

Old time lightkeepers were often an inventive lot. To provide his family with transportation, keeper Louis Bouchan of St. Martin Island, Lake Michigan, brought this Ford Model T out to the island piece by piece, then reconstructed it. Bouchan Collection.

desolate place, or in the middle of a busy harbor. Each location also calls for a different type of light and structure.

Educating the keeper's children was frequently a problem. If possible, the Service tried to station the keeper near enough to a school but many times this wasn't possible. However it is apparent the Service expended every effort to transfer keepers with families to lights near schools. A frequent solution when schools were not available, was to board the children with a family in town. Such expenses of course were paid by the keeper, not the government.

Keepers also maintained careful logbooks of the weather, vessels passing the station and other items of daily activity. Inspectors admonished the keepers if they became too flowery or personal in their entries. After all, it was an official government journal, not a diary!

A lighthouse was often a family enterprise where the husband and wife teamed up to make the light a success. The husband as keeper assumed full responsibility for the light proper, while the wife took charge of the dwelling. The children pitched in where they could too. Everyone worked to, "keep the light."

The feared inspector was supposed to arrive unannounced, but the Service version of the, "jungle telegraph" usually gave the keepers adequate warning. When telephones were finally installed at the isolated stations a friendly call from someone at headquarters generally gave fair warning that the inspector was on his way. When a Lake Michigan inspector tried driving to some of the closer stations by car, friends of the keepers also gave warning. When the inspector left the main highway and turned down the gravel road to the station someone with a telephone inevitably spotted him and called the local keeper giving him enough time for a final brush-up. If he was arriving by tender and the day was foggy, the distinctive sound of the vessel's engines gave away it's presence. In clear weather the inspector's pendant was visible on the mast.

Once the inspector was spotted, the station crew went into a flurry of activity. Last minute dusting and cleaning, straightening up and polishing were the order of the hour. Children hurried to put away toys and help wherever possible. The keeper donned his best uniform and family their Sunday best. If the inspector had a weakness for hot apple pie or other baked goods, the wife did her best to whip up a fresh batch.

Lighthouse inspectors often used this husband-wife team effort to their advantage. After carefully examining the husband's light, he would pull the man aside and say something to the effect that he was doing a fine job but that his wife was letting him down. She just wasn't keeping the quarters up to standard. Perhaps the keeper could encourage her to do a better job. When he finished checking the quarters, the inspector would pull the wife aside and tell her the same thing about the husband's performance. Such a management method doubtless led to interesting family discussion as the inspector's yawl pulled away from the dock.

In the early days, keepers often moonlighted with other jobs as a way of supplementing the poor pay. Fishing, farming and lumbering were popular sidelines to their official duties. As the Service matured, such practices were forbidden.

In the 1880's, Nathaniel Fadden, the keeper at Lake Superior's Manitou Island, Michigan, reportedly operated a still at the lighthouse that produced an especially powerful strain of rot-gut whiskey. Producing booze at the light was bad enough, but he apparently also sold it to the local Indians. Since Manitou Island, just off the tip of the Keweenaw Peninsula, was about as remote as you can get, his activities were not easily seen. Things got out of hand in 1886, when arguments over price and quality resulted in a farcical Indian attack on the light. When the situation was finally understood by the authorities, Fadden was dismissed and jailed.

Pay was always a source of complaint. Sometimes the complaints were even listened to! The keeper of Gayhead Light in 1805, made this partition for an increase in salary.

"Sir: Clay and Oker of different colours from which this place derived its name ascend in a Sheet of wind pened by the high Clifts and catch on the light House Class, which often requires cleaning on the outside - tedious service in cold weather, and additional to what is necessary in any other part of the Massachusetts.

"The Spring of water in the edge of the Clift is not sufficient. I have carted almost the whole of the water used in my family during the last Summer and until this Month commenced, from nearly one mile distant.

"These Impediments were neither known nor under Consideration at the time of fixing my Salary.

"I humbly pray you to think of me and (if it shall be consistent with your wisdom) increase my Salary.

"And in duty bound I am your's to Command."

Ebenezer Skiff
Keeper of Gayhead Light House

After considering the request, President Jefferson increased his salary by $50 to $250 per year. An additional complaint by Skiff ten years later to the Commissioner of Revenue brought another $50 increase.

Some keepers performed remarkable feats as a matter of course. The keeper of post lights on the St. Johns River, Florida, described one such incident. "I arrived at the light at 9:30 a.m. I took the lamp out and as I went to blow it out it exploded and knocked me off the light (twenty-two feet), and I did not know anything until 12 noon. When I came to I found the lamp gone. I crawled back to the boat two hundred and fifty feet, got another lamp and put it on the beacon and lite it. Then came home (eight miles). Injury: broken leg just above the ankle and severe bruised shin and bruised arm and lick on head."

An old time keeper on the Columbia River, Oregon demonstrated another kind of loyalty. He took only two days of leave in twenty-three years and one of the two days was used for his marriage!

Perhaps the best example of devotion to duty was exhibited by the keeper of a Hudson River lighthouse. When the tower was struck by a bolt of lightning, he was knocked out of his chair and temporarily paralyzed, but still stayed on duty until daybreak. These old keepers were certainly a tough bunch of birds!

Lightkeeping was a job constantly in transition. From the free-wheeling days of the Fifth Auditor to the tight control of the Coast Guard, requirements, procedures and technology continued to evolve. The tales of the men and women that kept the lights now are only remembered in the old logbooks, yellowed news clippings and fading memories of the few old-time keeps still left. The colorful and exciting era of lightkeeping is dead but hopefully not forgotten.

Footnotes:

1. *Coast Guard Bulletin*, February 1940.

2. Frederick Talbot, *Lightships and Lighthouses* (Philadelphia: J.B. Lippincott Company, 1913), p. 34.

3. Letter from Stephen Pleasonton to John P. Kennedy, Chairman, Committee on Commerce, U.S. House of Representatives, December 28, 1841, NARA, RG 26.

References:

Hans Christian Adamson, *Keepers of the Lights* (New York: Greenberg, 1955), pp. 319-335.

Annual Report of the Lighthouse Board (Washington, DC: US Department of the Treasury, various issues).

Thomas Appleton, *Usque ad Mare, A History of Canadian Coast and Marine Services* (Ottawa: Department of Transportation, 1968), pp. 105-111.

"A Brief History of Canadian Lighthouses," [*http://members.aol*.com/stiffcrust/pharos/index.html#imperial]. November 5, 1997.

"Canada's Georgian Bay", [*http://www.biddeford*.com/lhdigest/sept96/georgia.html]. October 28, 1997.

Captain Walter C. Capron, *The U.S. Coast Guard* (New York: Franklin Watts, Inc., 1965), pp. 121-127.

Mike Van Hoey, "Lights of the Straits," *Michigan History Magazine*, September/October, 1986, pp. 24-25.

Francis Ross Holland Jr., *America's Lighthouses, An Illustrated History* (New York: Dover Publications, 1988), pp. 1-54.

Instructions to Light-Keepers (Allen Park: Michigan: Great Lakes Lighthouse Keepers Association, 1989).

Barry James and Grant Day, *History and Archaeology of the First Copper Harbor Lighthouse*, Report of Investigations Number 21 (Archaeology Laboratory, Department of Social Sciences, Michigan Technological University, Houghton Michigan, 1995), pp. 5-32; 99.

Arnold B. Johnson, *The Modern Lighthouse Service* (Washington, DC: 1890), pp. 17-19.

Robert Erwin Johnson, *Guardians of the Sea, History of the United States Coast Guard, 1915 to the Present* (Annapolis, Maryland: Naval Institute Press, 1987), pp. 161-163.

Letter from Stephen Pleasonton to John P. Kennedy, Chairman, Committee on Commerce, U.S. House of Representatives, December 28, 1841, NARA, RG 26.

"Lighthouses." [http://www.tesarta.com/www.resources/library/lighthouse.html] November 27, 1999.

National Maritime Initiative, *1994 Inventory of Historic Light Stations* (Washington, DC: US Department of the Interior, National Park Service, 1994).

Donald L. Nelson, correspondence to author, March 9, 1996.

George R. Putnam, *Lighthouses and Lightships of the United States* (New York: Houghton Mifflin Company, 1917), pp. 185-193; 196; 203; 231-232; 237-239.

Wayne Sapulski, "The Imperial Towers," *Great Lakes Cruiser*, pp. 25-29.

Talbot, Frederick A., Lightships and Lighthouses (Philadelphia: J.B. Lippincott Company, 1913), pp. 29-31; 33-37;42-48; 209-210.

U.S. Department of Commerce, Lighthouse Service, *The United States Lighthouse Service, 1915* (Washington, DC: Government Printing Office, 1916), pp. 32-37; 40-56; 60-64; 73-77; 81-83.

George Weiss, *The Lighthouse Service, It's History, Activities and Organization* (Baltimore: The Johns Hopkins Press, 1916), pp. 4-10.

A.B.C. Whipple, *The Whalers* (Alexandria, Virginia: Time-Life Books, 1979), pp. 155-157.

THE KEEPERS

II

Joshua Appleby The Wrecking Keeper

Territorial Florida in the 1820s-1840s was very much a rough and rugged frontier. The men and women who moved through its history were a varied lot. Some were citizens, good and true, working hard to settle the new land, to build a solid future for themselves and their children. Others were a bit more "shady," willing sometimes to tread the thin line between honesty and dishonesty. Joshua Appleby appears to have been such a man. In the end though, Joshua Appleby held to his post as lighthouse keeper and paid for his stubbornness with his life. It is well his courage is remembered in the US Coast Guard cutter *Joshua Appleby*. May she serve with as much tenacity as he did!

The rocks and shoals of the Bahama Islands and Florida Keys formed a natural ship trap. A great reef, sometimes ranging 50 miles wide, ran between the Bahamas and Keys. In some places the deadly coral was hardly a foot below the surface. Between the reefs and keys, there was a narrow channel of safe water 200 miles in length, and through it ran an incredible amount of commerce. Great Spanish galleons, coastal traders, British vessels from the Bahamas, New England fishing schooners and black-flagged pirates–all used the narrow passage to reach and depart the ports of Cuba, South America and the Gulf of Mexico. The confined channel caused the water to flow fast, and strong currents could push vessels on to the sharp reefs on even windless days. Poor if any charts, no navigational aids such as lighthouses, and powerful hurricanes, all added to the danger. The toll of shipwrecks in the area was large and their hulls lay rotting in the sun. Florida was a dangerous place, in both fair weather and foul.

During this tumultuous time, both South American republics of Columbia and Venezuela commissioned privateers to fight against the hated Spanish. A considerable number of these ships were manned by American captains and crews. After the successful conclusion of the War of 1812 against Great Britain, many American sailors were without work. A successful privateering voyage against the Spanish could mean a good living for the otherwise unemployed men and many signed on for the opportunity. While Letters of Marque allowed them to capture only Spanish vessels, when the pickings were lean, sometimes such niceties were easily forgotten.[1]

Following the American Revolution, many Loyalists fled to Florida, then a British territory, as well as Jamaica and Bermuda. It didn't take the displaced Loyalists long to realize that there was money to be made salvaging the wrecks and thus was born the profession of "wrecking."

The large vessel traffic spawned nefarious characters and on December 6, 1821, a St. Augustine grand jury petitioned the court that "…the situation of the Florida Keys that harbors contiguous thereto have become the resort of wreckers and pirates and would respectfully suggest to the General Government the propriety and utility of stationing a naval and military force in that neighborhood, for the purpose of suppressing those disorders." [2]

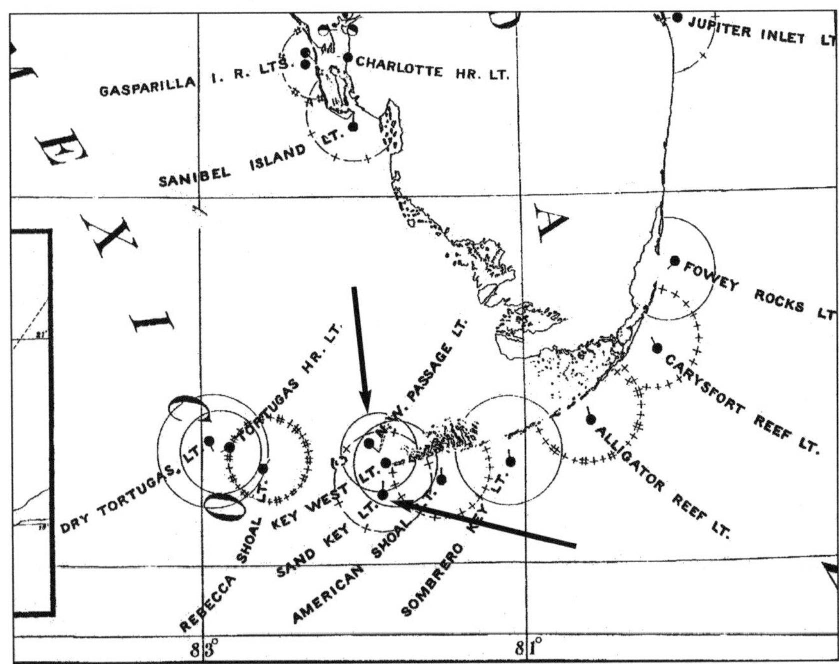

Responding to the complaints of mariners, on May 18, 1826, Congress authorized the construction of a lighthouse on Sand Key. The key was described as a "small, low lying spit of sand nine miles south southwest from Key West." Key West is at the extreme south end of the Florida Keys and is the most southern city in the United States. Sand Key is near the entrance of the southwest channel leading to Key West. Although its size varied with the whim of the sea, during Appleby's time the spit itself measured a bare 150-200 yards long and 50 yards wide. Proposals were duly advertised for, and on July 29, Stephen Pleasonton, the Fifth Auditor of the Treasury Department and head of the US Lighthouse Service, awarded a contract for the construction of the lighthouse and fitting out of the tower with appropriate apparatus. As was the current practice in the early days of the Lighthouse Service, the Collector of Customs at Key West was instructed to oversee construction. The light was similar in design to those at Cape Florida, Key West, and Garden Island at the Dry Tortugas.

The contract stipulated a round stone or brick tower, 65 feet high, 25 feet in diameter at the base, and 12 feet at the top. Walls at the base were five feet thick, and two feet at the top. Lantern height was to be 70 feet above sea level. A keeper's house, cook house, privy and cistern were also included in the contract.

Firmly anchoring a light tower to the ground is always critically important. On mainland headlands, or rocky islands, it is a relatively easy job. If properly constructed, the lighthouse will remain solid throughout the worst of storms. On offshore reefs, it is more difficult, but still well within engineering capability. With proper cofferdams and attention to good construction practice and materials, the tower will stand firm for a very long time, often a century or more.

When the tower must be built on sand, it is an entirely different story. Beach erosion can result in a tower, once safely distant from the breakers, to gradually become exposed as the waves sweep the beach away. Constructing tower on an offshore sand spit was usually a recipe for disaster.

The first keeper was John Flaherty. He had been the keeper at the Dry Tortugas Light, 70 miles to the west of Key West. Apparently his wife, Rebecca, had difficulty coping with the utter and complete remoteness of the Tortugas. A native of Frederick City, Maryland, and used to a semblance of civilization, the desolation of the Tortugas was just too much for her to stand.

On April 15, 1827, the light at Sand Key was illuminated for the first time. The apparatus consisted of 11 lamps with 15-inch reflectors, giving an estimated range of 13 miles. As normal, the infamous Winslow Lewis was the supplier. Since nearby Key West was a fixed light, the one at Sand Key was established as a revolving one.

The lighthouse was remote and getting adequate supplies to it could be dangerous. When the rains didn't come and the cisterns were empty, special shipments of water had to be made just to keep the lightkeepers alive.

Shortly after assuming his new duties, Flaherty became ill and went north for medical treatment. Rebecca was appointed in his place as a substitute keeper. After his death in 1830, she became keeper in her own right. To help combat the loneliness, her sister moved in with her.

In the nearly womanless frontier of Territorial Florida, the female keepers of Sand Key Light were likely a highly-sought-after commodity. Male visitors were common on the lonely key. Local fisherman and wreckers also often stopped to see how the two women were getting on at their lonely citadel. Contemporary accounts relate that in good weather, the island became a popular place for picnic parties from Key West. In November, 1834, Rebecca Flaherty married a Captain Frederick Neill. The ceremony was conducted at the lighthouse. Whether he was one of the visitors or someone she had known previously, isn't known.

Whether it was at Rebecca's request or an official recognition that there was now a man at the light, Frederick Neill was appointed keeper. But their life at Sand Key was to be short. Probably both Rebecca and Frederick were lonely for the civilization of the north because on February 10, 1836, he resigned as keeper and Captain Francis Watlington was appointed to succeed him. Watlington didn't last long. On July 27 of that year Captain Joshua Appleby was appointed keeper.

Appleby was born in Rhode Island on December 5, 1773. Like many boys of the "Ocean State," he went to sea at a very young age. He later married a woman named Sara Vial but she died at age 23, leaving him with a year-old daughter, Emily. By 1820, he had remarried, now to Mary Forester. About that time he also made his first trip to Florida. Recognizing the potential of the southern frontier, he decided to settle permanently on Key Vaca, about 37 miles north of Key West.[3]

In November 1822, he and a partner, John W. Fiveash of Norfolk, Virginia, started operating a ship replenishment station they named Port Monroe on Key Vaca. Four months later the pair placed a notice in the Floridian newspaper which said in part, "Immediately at the west end of the key is the settlement, where there is a flag staff erected. This port has …boats and provisions of all kinds to relieve those who may be so unfortunate as to get on the Florida Reef.... At present there are four families residing at this place: corn, potatoes, beans, onions, cotton and all West Indian fruit thrives rapidly." Appleby also worked as a fisherman and turtler. Green turtles were an important source of food. They were common in the area and could be easily caught and kept alive aboard a vessel, providing a constant source of fresh meat in the days before refrigeration. Some sailors compared the taste to veal.

Business must have been good since, on February 20, 1824, a correspondent advocated placing a customs officer on Key Vacas because of the "great number of English wreckers that cruise and rendezvous in that area." [4]

Previous to Florida being ceded to the United States in 1821, wreckers carried their salvage to the Bahamas or Cuba, the most convenient points with a good market. Until the U.S. Government acted forcibly to halt this activity, it continued with considerable loss to the Government in taxes and fees, thus there was great argument over where to establish a customs office and how to regulate U.S. wreckers and exclude foreign ones.

Appleby was also a wrecker. Wreckers in the Florida Keys , especially Key West, were both saints and sinners. When a ship ran up on a reef, in fair weather or foul, the wreckers went to her immediate aid and either assisted in the salvage of the cargo, or in some instances, stole the cargo outright. There were occasions when business was slow, that Florida wreckers were accused of causing wrecks by displaying false lights to lure vessels into the reefs. The wreckers then murdered anyone left alive and plundered the cargo. Appleby, however, was never accused of such terrible deeds and certainly such men were in the minority.

The Florida Keys teemed with wreckers and Key West was the heart of activity. The centerpiece of the local economy was wrecking. Nearly every citizen was involved in the business in some fashion.

Key West started in 1822, when an enterprising American, John W. Simonton, recognizing the opportunity for a wrecking station in Florida, purchased the land that later became Key West. Simonton worked fast. By the end of the year, the city was an official port of entry complete with a customs inspector. The nearest other customs port was at St. Augustine, 400 miles to the north. Soon, industrious seamen from New England, also appreciating the great opportunities Key West offered, established operations there. Some worked as wreckers, others as fishermen and merchants. Buying and selling wrecked ships and salvaged cargoes became the order of the day. Within a short period permanent houses were built and piers for unloading the ships and warehouses for storing recovered cargoes were constructed. The city grew steadily and by 1830, the population was 517. By 1835, there were 20 good-sized wrecking schooners working out of the city and a host of smaller craft. The harbor was deep enough for the largest vessels and prevailing winds allowed easy coming and going.

Key West was very much a frontier town. Bars lined the streets, and wreckers, divers, spongers, turtlers, fishermen, ship chandlers, sailmakers, saloon-keepers, shipwrecked sailors and merchants all mingled freely in the new town. When news of a shipwreck reached the town, a large bell was rung to alert all of the news. Immediately men came running for their ships in a race to be first at the wreck.

In the absence of an Admiralty Court, which was necessary to determine wrecker's fees, a local council passed a resolution establishing "wrecker's courts." Such courts allowed a Justice of the Peace or Notary to select a jury of five disinterested men who would decide the proper compensation due the wrecker. While this unique arrangement was in force, it gave wreckers the ability to literally plunder wrecks under the thin veneer of the law. The "wreckers courts" remained in force until May 23, 1828, when a Federal Superior Court was established at Key West. The court was also given the job of licensing wreckers. Wreckers' licenses could be revoked for stealing wrecked goods, grounding a vessel under the guise of piloting her, or making illegal promises or payments to the vessel master. In spite of the court's oversight, there certainly were instances of illegal acts. Some were discovered, others were not.

Payment of salvage, as determined by the judge, was a reward based on compensation for services, and included intangibles such as personal danger faced by the wrecker, the danger the cargo and vessel were in, the amount of labor and skill used by the wrecker, and the value of the vessel and cargo. Of course, if neither vessel or cargo were saved, the wrecker received nothing. Good intentions brought no reward!

The courts gave no reward for saving human life. This was done as a matter of course and the full hospitality of Key West was extended to the victims. The courts were indeed busy. Between 1848-57, four hundred ninety-nine vessels were disposed of by the courts at Key West. Total wrecks are not included in this count. Once the judge rendered his verdict, vessel and cargo were usually sold at auction, with the proceeds used to repay salvage costs.

By 1850, it was said Key West was the richest community per capita in the United States. There were 650 houses in the city and 50 vessels in the wrecking fleet.

Unlike wreckers in the New England states where they waited in port for news of a wreck, the Florida wreckers patrolled the reefs daily. Some ships cruised the reefs for months on the wrecking grounds, all the time looking for salvage. The potential for mishap was high. One old Key Wester claimed 100-150 square riggers entered or left the channel daily.

The problem of Bahamian wreckers "poaching" in U.S. territory was a constant one. The Collector of Customs at Pensacola wrote the following to the Secretary of the Treasury in a November, 1821 letter:

> ...part of the coast... is at present the rendezvous of a number of individuals emphatically called wreckers: There are at present, as I am informed by the Master of an American Vessel lately entered here from that coast, about forty sail employed in prosecuting that business as a profession, the commanders of which openly own their intention to continue on that ground until they shall be ordered off by the authorities of the U.S. of which they expressed themselves the belief they should shortly have efficient notice: They will not probably be allowed much longer to continue to find facilities in prosecuting that business within the jurisdiction of the U.S. The property of the vessels in that employ is for the most part said to belong to British merchants.[5]

Two years later, another writer said:

> I have been very credibly informed that there are 120 Sail of Vessels, kept employed from the Bahama Islands, within the Carysford Reef, whose Sole employment is wrecking and Transporting over to Providence, Goods of this description, and that the Amount of duties, paid to the British Government in Nassau by those Wreckers, may be fairly estimated at 15,000 pounds yearly. This Trade had been enjoyed by the inhabitants of the Bahama Islands, Since the first Settlement of those Keys - they appear to Consider it as their right, and are determined to preserve in it, until our Government, by the adoption of Some energetick (SIC) Measures, Shall Compel them to withdraw.[6]

In March 1825, Congress finally passed an act barring non-U.S. ships from wrecking in U.S. waters. In response, many of British wreckers just moved to Key West. What was the small matter of nationality when there is a wreck in the offing?

In another letter to the Secretary of the Navy, a correspondent advocated the establishment of a marine hospital:

> There are probably four or five hundred Mariners engaged on this coast wrecking and fishing (who like all other sailors, I believe it a characteristic trait) are remarkable for their improvidence and reckless disregard of future events. Those engaged in the wrecking business sometimes receive several hundred dollars as prize money which they usually spend in riotous dissipation and whilst doing so, they contract malignant diseases peculiar to this climate... a number of these destitute creatures have died for want of the most ordinary assistance.[7]

Key West was however, distant from the worst (or best) location for wrecks, the Carysfort Reef area, two or three days sail to the north. By contrast, Appleby's Key Vaca was much closer to the action, thus his hopes for the future were high.

In April, 1824, in an effort to expand business, Appleby and a partner opened a store on nearby Indian Key. The customers were not only wrecking crews but also settlers and local Indians. Perhaps most important, Indian Key also had a freshwater spring, a rare commodity along the desolate keys.

Appleby appears to have been a thinking man, always ready to look at new ways to make a profit. In February 1823, the Colombian privateer *La Centella* arrived off Port Monroe. John Fiveash piloted her into the anchorage where her captain, one Charles Hopner, offered Appleby a proposition. While of very dubious legality, it had the potential for great profits. Appleby was immediately interested.

Captain Hopner explained the opportunity thus. Under the strict conditions governing privateering, all captured prize vessels were to be returned to the country issuing the commission. In the case of the *La Centella*, this was Columbia, a thousand miles away from the best hunting grounds off Florida. On arrival in Columbia a prize court would eventually condemn the vessel and sell the cargo, crediting the profit to the privateer's account. All of this was both slow and expensive. Months could pass before the privateer or her crew received any money and the opportunity for official graft was high.

Hopner suggested a unique solution to the problem. Rather than send his prizes back to Columbia, he would bring them to Key Vaca where Appleby would assess the cargo and give the privateer captain a promissory note for the value and a healthy profit. Hopner would then carefully "wreck" the vessel on a nearby reef. Wrecker Appleby would then salvage the cargo and vessel, sell both and pay off the note. Salvage is always easier on a "non-wreck" If the two men worked together, the opportunity for profit was great!

How many prizes were processed in this unorthodox manner isn't known, but in April, 1823, a major stumbling block appeared in the form of Commodore David Porter of the U.S. Navy. Porter was appointed on February 1, 1823, to command the West Indian Squadron and directed to suppress piracy and protect American citizens and commerce in the area. He further was to establish a supply base at Key West. Stated somewhat more plainly, Florida now had a sheriff!

In May and June Hopner delivered two more prize vessels to Appleby, who following their agreement, issued promissory notes to the privateer captain. Before the prizes could be disposed of however, two Spanish citizens from Havana reached Key West and asked Porter for the return of their vessels. Porter acted quickly, perhaps seeing this activity as part of the piracy he was tasked to stamp out. First he wrote to the Secretary of the Navy for instructions, saying in part:

> I am under the impression that the practice of wrecking Spanish vessels on our coast by Colombian cruisers, in order to secure their cargoes, has, for a long time past, been pursued to a considerable extent, and that the establishment at Key Vacas was made with object chiefly in view.
>
> I feel myself somewhat at a loss how to act in this business, which appears to be one of peculiar delicacy. I thought that the first proper step was to remove all cause of suspicion and complaint from the authorities of Cuba, reserving to myself the right of acting as circumstances might hereafter make necessary.
>
> I beg your early instructions on this subject both as regards the disposal of the property and the course I ought to pursue toward the cruiser, (which claims the character of a Government vessel) if she should be elected and the individuals (aiders and abettors) residents at Key Vacas.
>
> As wrecking on this coast is a business of great importance and extensively carried on, I should be glad to be informed whether there are any laws to regulate it. Previous to my coming here, the neighboring keys were much frequented by English wreckers who took the property to New Providence…[8]

Not waiting for a reply to his letter which could take months, Porter immediately sent a letter to Appleby ordering him not to dispose of any of the promissory notes until legal ownership was determined. When Porter learned that one of the settlers at Port Monroe had been killed by a Spanish fisherman, reacted immediately sending a squad of marines to arrest Appleby and seize the vessels and cargo in question. Appleby was sent to Charleston, South Carolina for trail.

The eventual reply Porter received from the Secretary of the Navy was not what he expected:

> I deferred replying to your communications, respecting the disposition of the wrecked property, that you deemed it your duty to take into Custody, until I could have the opportunity of submitting the matter to the consideration of the President of the United States, who was at the time your letter was received, absent on a visit to Virginia.
>
> There can be no doubt, from the representations you have made, that the wreck was fraudulent and that method adopted to supersede, as was

> supposed, the necessity of proceedings in a court of Admiralty, to try the question of prize. There is no statue of the United States regulating the disposition of property wrecked on our territory; but the common law contemplates all wrecks as the property of the Sovereign. The proper course will, therefore, be to send the whole of the property to St. Augustine and have it placed in the custody of the Marshal; carefully preserving all the writings and papers found with the same, which you will transmit to the Attorney of the U.S. for East Florida, with a request that he will institute proceedings against the property in the Superior Court of East Florida, on behalf of the United States, founded on the right of the United States to the said property as wreck and given notice to all parties interested to appear and interpose their respective claims.
>
> As regards the conduct of Joshua Appleby, detained under arrest, it is not expedient to institute any further proceedings; his offense does not amount to a positive violation of any law of the United States, you will therefore, direct him to be forthwith liberated.[9]

In today's parlance, it would appear Appleby escaped on a "technicality."

Appleby returned to Key Vacas to continue his enterprise. For a while business boomed, with enough wreckers and fishermen using Port Monroe to cause the Customs agent at Key West to ask for a Customs Office to be established there, since the vessels were entering and departing illegally. In a February 20, 1824, letter he wrote, "I would further state, that it appears very necessary that an Inspector should be appointed to reside at Key Vacus, owing to the great number of English wreckers that cruise and rendezvous in that neighborhood...."[10]

Another Customs Collector had earlier complained in a May 21, 1823, letter that a revenue cutter was needed: "By placing the Revenue Cutter under the command of the inspector, he would be able to prevent the British Wreckers from taking those goods out of the United States - before duties were secured. This trade has been injoyed by the inhabitants of the Bahama Islands, since the first settlement of those keys - they appear to consider it as their right and are determined to persevere in it..."[11] However, when the Bahamian wreckers were excluded in 1825, Port Monroe began to slide into oblivion.

Just as the unfortunate affair with the piracy problem seemed behind him, the promissory notes returned to haunt Appleby. Hopner demanded payment and the courts backed up his claim. Since Appleby was unable to sell the cargo from the "wrecked" ships as prohibited by Porter, he had no money to pay Hopner. Appleby tried to get Porter's support, arguing that he was only complying with the Commodore's directives, but to no avail. When the case went to trial, Appleby lost and was ordered to pay Hopner $7,112. With his fortunes at a low ebb, Appleby returned to Newport, Rhode Island.

Perhaps after a couple of harsh New England winters, he knew where he wanted to spend the rest of his life, because in 1830, he moved to Key West with his family and became the owner of the wrecking schooner *Mary Ann*. Since wrecking captains were required to be licensed by the Federal Court at Key West, the issuance of one to Appleby in effect cleared his name. He was thought of highly enough that in May 1832, he was one of 48 citizens petitioning for the appointment of one Theodore Owns as U.S. Marshall for the Southern District of Florida.[12] In 1835, he was one of 43 petitioners for a light at the North West passage into Key West.[13] Personal misfortune, however, continued to dog him. In 1833, his second wife died.

Perhaps the wrecking business wasn't as lucrative as he had hoped, or he wanted a more stable income, but on July 27, 1837, he sought and was appointed keeper of the Sand Key Light. It is interesting to note that Sand Key Light was built partially at recommendation of his old nemesis, Commander Porter, who early recognized the importance of a light in that location.

Regardless of his previous occupation, people said Appleby proved to be a good lightkeeper. The light always showed as bright as the primitive Winslow Lewis apparatus allowed and was a reliable beacon for sailors. The fall of 1837 was an especially bad year for hurricanes. While none struck Key West directly, the general storm conditions caused significant erosion at Sand Key. Pleasonton asked Congress for money to stabilize the lighthouse, but none was approved. In 1840, the old 11-inch reflectors were replaced with new 14 new lamps with 21-inch reflectors, somewhat improving the light's visibility.

Another hurricane slammed into the keys on September 4, 1842, passing between Key West and Havana. A great deal of destruction was done to Sand Key. The powerful winds destroyed the keeper's house and half of the actual island was swept away. The lanterns were also damaged. New reflectors and glass were eventually provided and a strong sea wall built to help prevent further erosion. Pending the construction of a new house, the keepers who still remained on the key likely lived in a simple canvas tent. House or no house, the job of keeping the light still had to go on! A new dwelling was soon built, but all in all, it was wasted effort. Another hurricane on October 3-4, 1844, struck the key with devastating power. Half of the island was again swept away, the new sea wall ruined and the keeper's house demolished. It was a year before the damage was repaired.

The life of a lighthouse keeper could be lonely and that of Joshua Appleby was no exception. To help overcome the loneliness, in early October, 1846, his daughter, Emily, and her second husband, Thomas Patterson, and their three year old son, Thomas, came to visit with him. Mrs. Mary Ann Petty, a friend from Newport, Rhode Island, and her young daughter, accompanied them. Whether this was intended to be just a short visit or a more permanent arrangement was uncertain. Their time at the lighthouse would be very brief. Mrs. Petty's relationship with Joshua wasn't clear. Was she an old "flame" from his Newport days he was courting, or just a friend of his daughters?

By the morning of October 11, it was obvious to everyone in the area that a hurricane was on the way. There was also nothing anyone could do but hunker down and try to ride it out. Running was out of the question. There wasn't anywhere to go! For those on the mainland there was some hope, but for the people on Sand Key, there was none. By noon the black storm roared in and pounded the area with such ferocity that one observer described it as "the most destructive of any that has ever visited these latitudes in the memory of man."[14]

The hurricane had spawned somewhere out in the Caribbean. It swept into Havana around midnight on October 10 and peaked at 0900 on the 11th. The devastation in Havana was truly awesome. Of 104 vessels in the harbor, all but a dozen were sunk or wrecked!

Winds in Key West began to increase on the morning of the 11th as the great hurricane inexorably bore down on the city. Lt. William C. Pease, aboard the Revenue Cutter *Morris* later wrote:

> The gale commenced about 10 o'clock on the 11th instant and about 2 P.M. it blew a perfect hurricane. I was on board the revenue cutter *Morris* about one mile from Key West at anchor with 150 fathoms of chain out, yards down on deck and every preparation made for the storm. Our riding bitts were working and it became necessary to back them with deck tackles, the current was now moving by us at the rate of 12 miles per hour: the *Morris* laying broadside to it as well as the wind, made her labor very heavy and in danger of parting her chains when we were compelled to cut away the mainmast for the safety of our lives as well as the vessel. When the mast went over the side it hung by the triaticc stay and in danger of falling on us every moment: a man could not get aloft and we were anxious to hold on the foremast as the last resort in case the schooner should founder at her anchors. After a few moments a man made out to get aloft and cut the stay when the mast fortunately fell clear of us.

> The sea made a complete breach over us. It was with difficulty we could keep her free with both pumps going and bailing from wardroom and birthdeck. At 4 p.m. the air was full of water and no man could look windward for a second. Houses, lumber and vessels drifted by us -- some large sticks of lumber turned end over end by the force of the current and the sea running so high and breaking over us brought lumber, casks, etc. on board of us across our decks. At quarter past four the water was up to our lowest half-ports inboard and gaining on us when our starboard chain parted and we commenced dragging we know not which way as our compasses flew around in such a manner that they became useless for that object. Now our fears were that we should go out over the reef and into the Gulf and before we got to the Gulf the vessel must strike and bilge: but that would not save her. At this time we cut away the foremast, when a sea struck us, knocking the schooner on her beam-ends, carrying away our bulwarks, cranes, larboard boat, quarter house, swinging boom and everything moveable off deck: and to right the vessel we hove the lee guns overboard and knocked out the ports -- all expecting momentarily to go to the bottom. We were in this suspense for about one hour, when we struck on some reef unknown, when our larboard chain parted and we made preparations to scuttle the vessel. The hurricane gradually subsided although at midnight we were sticking heavy and blowing a gale from the S.E.

Looking at Key West, Lt. Pease continued, "All the wharves are washed away or injured–not one warehouse escaped the fury of the storm–wood and stone seemed alike going to destruction. There are not 6 out of 600 houses but are unroofed or blown down."

An officer on board the U.S. Navy brig *Perry* also in the harbor reported that "Every vessel in the harbor is either sunk or driven ashore and most melancholy of all, more than forty lives have been lost.... As yet there have been more than 20 wrecks heard from and the loss of life truly lamentable. But no vessel could have lived in that storm without foundering or running ashore."

The hurricane continued to rampage up the east coast of the United States causing extensive damage over the Middle Atlantic states and western New England before finally blowing itself out.

When the weather finally calmed enough for Key West sailors to venture out, they discovered that Sand Key was gone, wiped off the face of the earth! The island, lighthouse dwelling had all disappeared without a trace. Where once the island and lighthouse stood, there was only empty water! There was a clear depth of six feet of water throughout the area! The bodies of those at the key were never found. Appleby had met his end as a lightkeeper should, at his post in the midst of a storm.

Lieutenant Pease further noted that, "...waves roll over the spot where Sand Key was. At Sand Key, six persons were killed or drowned, most likely the former, as the general impression is that they fled to the stone lighthouse for refuge, the key being very low. Poor old Captain Appleby, I knew him very well: he told me the first hurricane would sweep all to destruction and alas, his prediction is verified."[15]

As a temporary replacement for the Sand Key Light, the 140-ton lightship *Honey* was brought down from New York. The *Honey* remained on station until 1853, when a new light finally became operational.[16] The *Honey* was no answer to the dangers of the Sand Key area. An insurance underwriter in Key West lamented that "The ...[ship] is an old one and the light miserable." He reported also that eight vessels had been driven ashore between May 1850 - August 1851, with a loss of $450,000, all for the want of a good light.

On March 3, 1847, Congress appropriated $20,000 for a new lighthouse. Additional funding was provided in 1848. Knowing the difficulty of building a conventional lighthouse on Sand Key, the engineers elected to use a unique "screw pile" design. When the iron work was completed by a South Carolina firm, lighthouse engineer I. W. P. Lewis went to Sand Key to erect the new tower. By now the currents had recreated Sand Key. Each of the iron foundation piles was eight inches in diameter and 13 feet in length. At the bottom of each was a two foot diameter cast iron flange. The construction crew laboriously bored each pile into the coral to a depth of 10 feet below the surface. A dozen exterior piles were placed through massive four-foot-diameter cast iron disks anchored to concrete pads. Operations were then suspended when funds ran out. The new light was being built during a very tumultuous period in U.S. Lighthouse history. The infamous reign of the Fifth Auditor was ending and that of the new and efficient Lighthouse Board was just beginning. But it took a while for the new board to organize and reach its administrative stride and such stoppages were to be expected.

Work on the Sand Key Light started again in January 22, 1853, after the screw pile light at Carysfort Reef to the northeast was finished. The engineer in charge of the Carysfort project was Lieutenant George Meade of the Army's Topographic Engineer Corps. As a major general, Meade would later lead victorious Union forces at the Battle of Gettysburg. He was immediately send to finish the Sand Key project. After a delay waiting for funds, Meade set to work.

The "new" screwpile lighthouse at Sand Key. U.S. Coast Guard photo.

The new screw pile system was designed to withstand the worst hurricane. The foundation was solid and even if the old island washed away again, the lighthouse would remain. All of the ironwork was well-braced and would resist the force of wind and wave. A keeper's house was built on top of the first series of piles, well above wave height. A collection system brought rain water into a large cistern, assuring an adequate supply of good water for the keepers. From the center of the tower, an enclosed stairway provided easy access to the lantern and watch rooms. The total construction cost was $101,520, making it a very expensive facility. On July 20, 1853, the Sand Key Lighthouse was officially put into operation. Instead of the old complicated parabolic reflector system, a new first order Fresnel lens was installed. The Fresnel greatly increased the light's range and intensity. The light remained operational throughout the Civil War, most likely because of the presence of the U.S. Navy at Key West.

What the seas give they also take away, and in October 1865, another hurricane again washed away Sand Key. The new lighthouse was damaged but withstood the tempest in generally good order. The screw piles kept the light firmly anchored and safe from the ravages of wind and sea. Periodic hurricanes continued to damage the light, but in each instance repairs were made and its beam continued to shine.

The old lighthouse was converted to acetylene gas and automated around 1932. In the 1950s it was converted to electricity provided by batteries and in 1967 the first order Fresnel was replaced with a small fourth order model. On November 12, 1989, a fire of unknown origin destroyed the old keepers quarters.[17]

Whether saint or sinner, Joshua Appleby was a man of his time. Freewheeling and enterprising in his business dealings, he was willing to risk all in an effort to build success and make a better life for his family. He was certainly a brave man, for wrecking was not a profession for the fainthearted. Appleby also had that quality known as "gumption." Knocked down again and again by fortune's turn, losing two two wives and going bankrupt at least once, he kept "getting up, dusting himself off," and coming back to try again.

Footnotes

1. Letter of Marque, a commission given by a government granting a vessel authority to attack an enemy's commerce or privateers, primarily to get their cargo.

2. Clarence Edwin Carter, *The Territorial Papers of the United States,* Volume XXIV, *The Territory of Florida* (Washington, DC: National Archives, 1977), p. 295.

3. Also known as Key Vacas and Key Vacus.

The Joshua Appleby *will be stationed in St. Petersburg, Florida, close to the waters Joshua Appleby knew so well. U.S. Coast Guard photo.*

4. Carter, *Territorial,* Volume XXII, p. 852.

5. Carter, *Territorial,* Volume XXII, pp. 684-685.

6. Carter, *Territorial,* Volume XXII, p. 682.

7. Carter, *Territorial,* Volume XXIV, pp. 277-278.

8. Carter, *Territorial,* Volume XXIV, pp. 705-706.

9. Carter, *Territorial,* Volume XXIV, p. 723.

10. Carter, *Territorial,* Volume XXIV, p. 852.

11. Carter, *Territorial,* Volume XXIV, p. 684.

12. Carter, *Territorial,* Volume XXIV, pp. 701-702.

13. Carter, *Territorial,* Volume XXV

14. Walter C. Maloney, *A Sketch of the History of Key West* (Newark, N.J.: Adventure Printing House, 1876). p. 41

15. *New York Daily Tribune,* November 2, 1846.

16. Willard Flint, *Lightships of the United States Government* (Washington, DC: Coast Guard Historian's Office, 1989). n.p.

17. Roger Bansemer, "Sand Key Lighthouse." [http://bansemer.cfnet.com/FL-lighthouses/Sand%20Key.htm]. February 1999; Sheppard, Birse, *Lore of the Wreckers* (Boston: Beacon Press, 1961), pp.112-116, 125, 134-138, 142-145, 153-165; Carter, *Territorial*, Volume XXII; Love Dean, *Lighthouses of the Florida Coast*, (Key West, Florida: Historic Florida Keys Foundation, Inc. 1992), pp. 73-88; Lighthouse Letter File, Sand Key Clipping File, RG 26, NARA; David M. Ludlum, *Early American Hurricanes,* (Boston: American Meteorological Society, 1963), pp.151-153; *Miami Herald,* November 14, 1989; U.S. Coast Guard Naming File; John Viele, *The Florida Keys, A History of the Pioneers,* (Sarasota, Florida: Pineapple Press, 1996), pp. 22, 25-31.

III

Ida Lewis Of Lime Island

Certainly the most famous of all the heroic female lightkeepers in the country was Ida Lewis of Lime Rock, off Newport, Rhode Island. She was born on February 25, 1842, in her father's home in Newport. She was the second of four children. Her mother's name was Idawalley Zorada and it was passed on to her, although friends shortened it to Ida.

Her father, Captain Horsa Lewis, had been a pilot with the Revenue Marine for 12 years, but transferred to the Lighthouse Service due to his failing health. In 1854, he was named keeper of the light at Lime Island, just

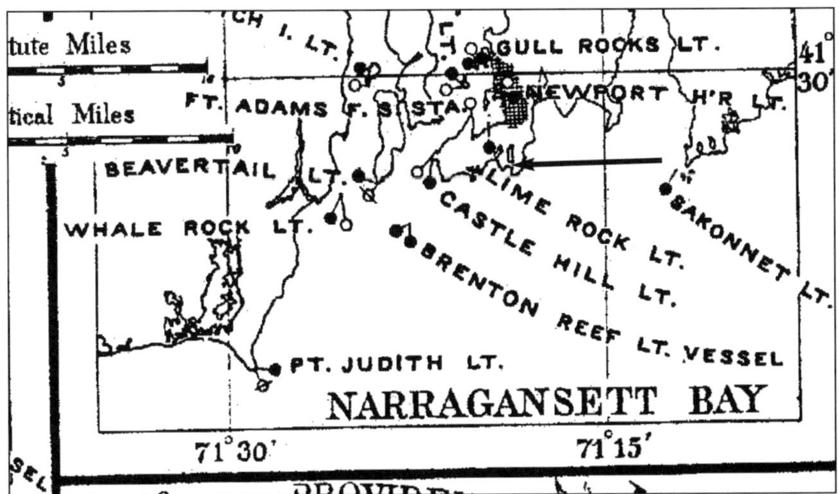

off Newport. At the time there was no quarters on the island for a family so they continued to live in the small wooden house on the corner of Spring and Brewer streets in Newport. Twice a day her father rowed out to Lime Island to light the lamp at dusk and extinguish it at dawn.

There are two versions to Ida's early life and the water. The first maintains that, as Ida grew up, she displayed a remarkable aptitude for the water. By the time she was 14 it is said she swam better than any person in Newport. She developed into an outstanding boat-handler. Frequently she helped fisherman or lobstermen, literally anything to keep her on the water. Often she rowed out to her father's lighthouse.

The second version claims she knew nothing about the sea or handling boats until she moved to the lighthouse. Then she took to it rapidly, becoming extremely skillful especially in rough water. It was said old-timers shook their heads in wonder as the daring Ida pulled sturdily through the foaming billows.

In the summer of 1858, when Ida was 15, her father moved the family into the new keeper's house built on the island. It was a simple square two story dwelling, perhaps even ugly. Downstairs was a parlor, dining room and hall, with an L-shaped kitchen below. On the upper floor were three bedrooms. The diminutive sixth order Fresnel lens was in the lantern room, attached to the side of the house.

Regardless of Ida's boat-handling skill, all around her was the sea and if she were to go anywhere, it would have to be by water. Four months after moving in, Captain Lewis suffered what apparently was a stroke. Although he recovered enough to sit up and eventually to hobble about with a cane, he was no longer able to keep the light. Ida's mother took over his duties while she assumed the jobs that involved boats. She rowed her sister and brother back and forth to school every day and went to Newport for supplies. Regardless of the weather, fair or foul, Ida handled the boat with consummate skill. Her father once remarked, "I have watched them until I could bear it no longer, expecting every moment to see them swamped and the crew at the mercy of the waves, and I know I have turned away and said to my wife, 'let me know if they get safe in,' for I could not endure to see them perish and realize we were powerless to save them." In addition, a seriously ill sister required attention. All of these new responsibilities left little time for Ida to receive a formal education. Before moving to the island, she had attended school regularly.

Ida's mother lived with Ida at the light until she died in 1887. Two of her three brothers died young, John in infancy and Horatio at age ten. Brother Horsea died at age thirty-four. Only her brother Rudolph outlived her. Her lone sister Hattie died at age thirty-two.

Lime Island Lighthouse. U.S. Coast Guard photo.

Ida's first rescue was in September, 1859, when she was 16. It seems that four young men, all sons of prominent Newport families, were sailing off the light when–in a fit of horseplay–one of the boys climbed the mast and rocked it back and forth until the motion capsized the boat. Ida saw the accident from the lighthouse and quickly launched her boat. Reaching the scene, she carefully hauled the boys about and returned with them to the light where she gave them a stiff dose of hot molasses. Since they did not wish to let their parents know what trouble they had caused, none of the boys ever mentioned the incident to them. It was 11 years before the rescue became public, and then only because of her later fame. Her father, however, witnessed the entire affair with his telescope.

It was eight years before Ida again performed a rescue. In February, 1866, three drunken soldiers from nearby Fort Adams were making their way back to the fort when they decided, instead of making the long walk, they would use a handy skiff they found at Jones Bridge. The fact that the skiff didn't belong to them and they would be stealing it, made no difference. Soon they were afloat and on their way to the fort. Two men were rowing while the third sat in the stern thumping his foot on the floor. Soon he sprung a plank and the boat started to sink. The two rowers swam for shore but the third hung grimly on to the sinking skiff. Ida saw the accident from the light and immediately rowed for the area. When she reached the skiff, it was plain the soldier was

An artist's rendition of her heroic rescue. U.S. Coast Guard collection.

A popular idea of Ida's home life. U.S. Coast Guard collection.

nearly finished, barely able to keep his head clear of the cold water. However, he was so drunk he was unable to help himself, and far too fat to be of much aid if he was sober. Unable to haul him into her boat, she rigged a bowline around him and towed him toward shore. After shouting for help, several men came out and pulled him to the beach where he was revived. The first two soldiers disappeared. Whether they drowned in their swim to shore or just took advantage of the opportunity to desert isn't clear.

In January 1867, Ida was again busy at the rescue business. Two local men were bringing a valuable sheep along a Newport street when it suddenly broke away and ran down a wharf and into the water. Desperate to recover the sheep, the three men got into a skiff and took off after it. Ida was sitting by a window in the lighthouse sewing when she noticed the men get into the boat, and since it was her brother's, she was curious what was going on–especially since a gale was blowing and the water was very rough. She was watching them when a large wave over turned the skiff, dumping them into the water. Again she launched her boat and rowed through tumbling seas to those in trouble. In no time at all, she had them aboard her craft then safely ashore. Not missing a beat, she rowed out and rescued the sheep for good measure!

A mere two weeks later, Ida's mother was looking out her window in the morning when she noticed a man stranded on Little Lime Rock, midway

Ida as a young woman.U.S. Coast Guard photo.

between the light and town. The waves were running high and a storm was clearly building. The man was clinging to the rocks with all his strength. Calling Ida to go to his aid, the mother shouted encouragement to the man. Within minutes Ida reached the man and brought him aboard her boat and landed him on the mainland. The man was not thankful at all to Ida and only later did she discover that he had stolen a small sailboat and then wrecked it on Little Lime Rock.

Ida as pictured in Harper's Weekly. *U.S. Coast Guard collection.*

A heavy gale was running on March 29, 1869, when her mother yelled to her, "Ida, Oh my Ida, run quick, a boat capsized and men are drowning! Run quick Ida!" Shoeless and without a coat or hat, she ran out into the storm, her younger brother following her. Before they reached the boat, one of the men had already drowned, but two others were still clinging to the overturned boat. All three were soldiers from the nearby fort. Carefully maneuvering the boat to bring her stern to the men, she brought both safely aboard and then back to the lighthouse. Had she let them try to come over the gunwhales, the boat surely would have capsized. Coming stern-to was a trick her father had taught her. After drying them out, she brought them to the fort. In thanks for her saving the men at the risk of her own life, the men of the fort sent Ida a letter of appreciation, an engraved silver teapot, and a purse containing $218 collected by the officers and men of the fort.

As rescue followed rescue, Ida's fame slowly grew. In recognition of her rescue of 11 people on May 1869, the Benevolent Society of New York awarded her a silver medal and $100. Other institutions also recognized her achievements. The *New York Tribune*, *Harper's* and *Leslie's* magazines ran articles on her brave rescues, and soon the entire nation knew about her. As the result of the tremendous publicity, Ida received large amounts of mail as well as marriage proposals and other "strange" offers.

On July 4, 1869, under fair skies and light breezes, the people of Newport held a parade in Ida's honor and presented her with a new lifeboat fittingly named *"Rescue."* The new boat was made of mahogany and adorned with velvet cushions and gold-plated hardware. The beautiful boat was mounted on a horse-drawn wagon. Ida was assisted into the boat, along with the orator who would formally present the boat, and a writer from the *Atlantic Monthly* who would give Ida's acceptance speech. The wagon was borne through town as if a royal procession. The presentation ceremony complete with long, flowery speeches, was held in Parade Park, near the Old State House in front of a huge and enthusiastic crowd. The people seemed to have "Ida on the brain." The boys wore "Ida Lewis" hats and ties and the girls knotted their scarfs as Ida did on a rescue. It is said she accepted the boat with modesty and humility. The Narragansett Boat Club presented Ida with an elegant rudder made of black walnut, finished with an inlaid plate of silver with an appropriate inscription. The officers of the steamer *Newport* presented her with two beautiful flags for the boat. When the celebration was finished, she simply stepped aboard her new boat and rowed back to the lighthouse. The crowd of thousands loved it and cheered loudly as her oars cut sharply into the water and made her way through the waves. In spite of the glitter of the

Music was even written about her exploits. U.S. Coast Guard collection.

Ida in her "Rescue." U.S. Coast Guard collection.

new boat, she preferred to use her old boat. It was "like herself, at once plain, commonplace and reliable."[1]

The Federal Government recognized her achievements with the award of the gold lifesaving medal. *The Annual Report of the U.S. Life Saving Service* had this to say:

> Under her maiden name of Ida Lewis, she has won a national celebrity by her early rescues. The papers accompanying the application made in her case to the Department show that she has saved from drowning thirteen persons, and that it is understood that the number is greater. The special instance upon which the medal was awarded, was her rescue, on February 4th (1881), of two soldiers belonging to the garrison at Fort Adams, near Newport, Rhode Island. These men were crossing on foot at 5 o'clock in the afternoon, or near twilight, between the fort and Lime Rock light-house, of which Mrs. Lewis-Wilson is the keeper and suddenly fell through the ice, which had become weak and rotten. Hearing their drowning cries, Mrs. Lewis-Wilson ran toward them from the light-house with a rope, and, in imminent danger of the soft and brittle ice giving way beneath her, and also of being dragged into the hole by the men, both of whom had hold of the line she had flung them, she succeeded in hauling first one, and then the other, out of the water. The first man she got out entirely unaided, her brother arrived and helped her with the second. The action on her part showed unquestioned nerve, presence of mind, and dashing courage. The ice

> was in a very dangerous condition, and only a short time afterward, two (other) men fell through and were drowned, while crossing in the night in the immediate neighborhood of the scene of the rescue. All the witnesses unite in saying that the rescue was accomplished at imminent risk of the rescuer's life.[2]

After her father died in 1872, Ida's mother was appointed keeper until 1879 when Ida was officially selected keeper in her place.

The nationwide publicity Ida had attracted with her daring rescues meant she would receive many visitors to the island. The June 20, 1870, issue of the *Boston Journal* estimated 10,000 people visited her the previous summer. "People would land at the rock, prowl over the house, quiz the family, try to pry into the household affairs, patronizingly ask the age of each person and what they lived on, and how they felt when Ida was saving souls."[3]

There are two versions to the visit of President Grant in August 1869. It the first it was said the President and Vice President Cox came to Lime Island to see her. As President Grant stepped ashore he got his feet wet and later was quoted as saying, "I have come to see Ida Lewis and to see her I'd get wet up to my armpits if necessary." Ida and the President had a long talk and she told him all about her life at the light and showed her the lighthouse. At the time, Ida was 28. Lewis fans claimed Grant later remarked that his time with Ida was one of the most interesting events in his life.

In the second version the President was unable to visit Lime Island so he asked her to come to town. Decked out in her holiday garb, she rowed *Rescue* to Long Wharf, where she found the Presidential party waiting in carriages while en route to the railroad station. General Grant received her and made a small speech to her on her success, saying "I am happy to meet you, Miss Lewis, as one of the heroic, noble women of the age."

Another pleasant episode was her reception on the Massachusetts school ship when it called in Newport harbor. Earlier the ship's officers had visited Ida on Lime Island. When she went to return the call to the ship, a boat met her before she reached the ship and took her under tow the remainder of the way. The apprentices lay aloft and manned the yards while the ships guns boomed a salute. After Ida toured the ship, she was treated to a chorus by the crew and a welcoming speech by the captain. When she departed, the crew again manned the yards and gave three cheers while the colors dipped in her honor.

Other notables also visited Ida's humble lighthouse. In 1907, she remarked, "... every Mrs. Astor and every Mrs. Vanderbilt and every Mrs. Belmont you ever heard of", had come to visit. She further mentioned these worthies came with "… whole boat loads of men and women that all talked at once and treated me as if I were a kind of real queen."

Ida also spoke at length of her plans for the summer.

> I've got to paint the whole house inside this year. That's Government work, so I do it myself… My brother–I let him do the outside work because I am getting old, I guess, and I really can't handle a boat like I used to.
>
> Sometimes the spray dashes against these window so thick I can't see out and for days at a time the waves are so high that no boat would dare come near the rock, not even if we were starving. But I am happy. There's a peace on this rock that you don't get on shore. There are hundreds of boats going in and out of this harbor in the summer, and it's part of my happiness to know they are depending on me to guide them to safety.
>
> For many seasons the Newport papers told of my excursions to this Light. My helpless father's chief occupation was to sit and count the number of visitors. Once he actually counted over six hundred in one day! In those times I shook hands with more people during a summer than did the President in Washington. I couldn't get my housework done. Hundreds from each state in the Union have been here, including men and women of the highest distinction. For example, there was Admiral Dewey. When he was Secretary of the Lighthouse Board he came here one day and said: "Miss Lewis, I want to smoke on your half-acre rock for half an hour."
>
> General William Tecumseh Sherman sat out on the rock for nearly an hour, asking me questions about my life, and saying he was glad to get to such a peaceful place. Yes, There's hardly a great admiral or noted general that hasn't been here to see me. There was one cabinet minister–the Secretary of the Treasury under Grant. He said he came purposely to thank me personally for saving the life of a soldier from Fort Adams, because the light was in his department and he was proud to have a woman in his department who was not finicky about getting her hair wet.

Ida never lost her sense of perspective. A reporter for the *Newport Daily News* visited Ida and reported, "Ida met us at the door, as different a being from what our expectations of a possibly over-flattered and consequently spoiled girl might have led us to anticipate. There was neither assumption nor affection in her manner. She apologized for her everyday work garb of plainest fashion and material, say frankly that she was trying to help mother get a little washing done. She talked pleasantly and without constraint, but unlike the world in general, seemed more fluent upon any theme than herself."[4]

Ida permitted a local Newport journalist to write a pamphlet about her exploits and to paint her portrait, copies of both of which were sold throughout the United States. As her fame spread, Ida received a stream of unsolicited attention. A Washington politician wrote asking for a lock of hair, and the State of Maine sent two gallons of maple syrup. A West Point cadet prevailed on his father to intercede with Ida on his behalf. In spite of his youth, he hoped Ida "… might learn to love him." A man from Missouri wrote asking to board at Lime Island over the summer. And a sailor sent her "personal verses":

Were thou but mine, those words
fall low and sweet.
Like the rich carol of that voice
of thine.
Then should our lips in tender passion
meet
And echo back the words, "were
thou but mine."

Ida, of course, was a magnet for all sorts of people with an "agenda" of their own. Susan B. Anthony, the great sufferaget visited her as a representative of the feminist movement and lectured her about being a model for other women to follow. Ida replied that she did not feel she was promoting feminism, but that she was simply doing her job. Anthony probably left disappointed.

In her later years Ida spoke about the creeping ravages of age. When questioned about the rescue of the soldiers through the ice, she said, "I was pretty strong then. It was hard work bringing those men out to strong ice, and it made my arms lame, but to-day I couldn't do it at all. Why , the other day, Rud–that's what we call by brother, you know (his name is Rudolph)–Rud asked me to help him lift a ladder, and he said to me, "You haven't got any more strength than a cat." I told him I was lifting all I could. But lately I haven't been feeling very well–nervous, you know. Maybe it's my heart. I don't know. But then I'm getting old." [5]

Ida accomplished her last rescue when she was 64. A friend was rowing out to the lighthouse when she inexpiably stood up in the boat, lost her balance and pitched into the sea. As in years past, Ida rushed to her boathouse and launched her lifeboat. Soon reaching the flailing woman, she hauled her aboard and returned to the lighthouse.

Ida was subjected to a barrage of visitors. U.S. Coast Guard photo.

In 1870, she married a Captain William Wilson, a fisherman and sailor of Black Rock, Connecticut. It was a brief union and they separated after two years. Questioned about it by a reporter, she simply indicated a mistake had been made, but she was rigidly opposed to divorce. She quoted, "What God has joined together, let no man put asunder." Details of this interesting period of her life are missing but it is easy to surmise the conflict between Ida's love of Lime Island and it's light and the demands of a new husband.

Ida suffered a stroke and later died at the lighthouse on October 24, 1911. She was 72 years old. During the three days she lay at the point of death, sympathy letters and telegrams poured in to Newport. So many flowers arrived, they could not all be sent to the lighthouse. Her brother believed the stroke was the result of what she perceived was criticism by the Lighthouse Service of her station operation. Rud had been her assistant for 25 years. Less than a month later, he resigned from the Lighthouse Service and left Lime Island forever. Ida had wisely been banking her Carnegie Fund pension money for Rud to provide for him when she died. Even in death she was taking care of her family. Up until her stroke, it was reported she was in excellent health, with "her cheeks tinged with color and eyes bright." It was reported that Fort Adams was having artillery practice at the time and the commander received a message that the guns were bothering Ida in her last moments. He duly suspended firing. A short time later Ida "passed over the bar."

Her funeral was a major event in Newport. Shops closed and flags flew at half staff on the morning of the funeral. The Thames Street Methodist Episcopal church was filled to overflowing. Ida joined the church about 1885, and tried to attend services once a day, weather permitting. A detail of six artillerymen acted as her pallbearers. The vessels in Newport Harbor tolled their bells in memory of the brave little lightkeeper. Her husband, William H. Wilson, never appeared for the funeral and his location was unknown.

During her 39 years as keeper, she was officially credited with saving 18 lives, although some reports claim as high as 25.

Ida received numerous awards for her rescues. Among them:

- U.S. Life Saving Service Gold Medal
- Massachusetts Humane Society Silver Medal
- American Cross of Honor Society Gold Medal
- Life Saving Benevolent Society of New York Silver Medal
- American Life Saving Society Silver Medal
- Gold Medal and Vote of Thanks From Rhode Island Legislature
- Life Pension From Carnegie Foundation

Ida was officially credited with saving 18 lives. U.S. Coast Guard photo.

- Gold Pin From the Sorosis Society of New York
- Silver Rudder Yoke and Boat Hook From Narragansett Boat Club
- Engraved Silver Teapot and Cash Purse From Officers and Men of Fort Adams
- Silk Pennant From Fall River Line
- Lifeboat From People of Newport
- Gold Plated Oarlocks From Jay Gould
- New Boathouse From Jim Fisk[6]

Ida kept her awards in a small workbasket she usually had in the kitchen. This was an example of the little value she placed on such "baubles."

Ida has often been called the "American Grace Darling." While such comparisons with the English heroine are valid, it must be remembered that Grace Darling made her rescue from the open sea while Ida did her's from the comparatively calm waters of Newport Harbor. When a subscription fund was started for the restoration of Grace Darling's tombstone in 1885, Ida was a contributor. She wrote to the English clergyman leading the drive, "Your work, a labor of love, should be crowned with success, and I fervently hope you will be able to raise all the funds necessary. I enclose my mite, which I trust, will be received."[7]

The tender Ida Lewis *being transported from the shop floor to the launch ways. She is the lead vessel in her class. Marinette Marine Corporation photo.*

An actress played the part of Ida Lewis at the launching to add a touch of history to the event. Marinette Marine Corporation photo.

Grace Darling was born in Bamburgh on November 24, 1815. When the lighthouse at Longstone Rock was built in 1826, her father became the keeper and moved his family there. On September 7, 1838, the steamship *Forfarshire*, carrying 60 passengers and crew bound from Hull to Dundee, experienced engine problems and struck a nearby reef. Some 43 people drowned in the wreck. Grace and her father used their boat to rescue nine people, found clinging to the rocks. From that day on, her life changed, with the word spreading through the press, gifts and medals arrived from all over the world. In 1842, her health rapidly declined and she died. An elaborate tomb was built at Bambaugh, Northumberland, United Kingdom.

In 1924, the Rhode Island legislature officially changed the name of Lime Rock to Ida Lewis Rock. Later the Lighthouse Service changed the name of the light to Ida Lewis Lighthouse. This was the only time a lighthouse was named to honor a former keeper. The old lighthouse is used by the Ida Lewis Yacht Club in Newport as a club house. In honor of Ida, its burgee carries 18 stars, one for each of her confirmed rescues.[8]

The Ida Lewis *underway on her trials. Marinette Marine Corporation photo.*

Footnotes

1. Ida's presentation boat is on display at the Newport Museum of Yachting at Fort Adams. The lighthouse lens can be seen at the new Museum of Newport History at the Brick Market.

2. *Annual Report U.S. Life Saving Service, 1881,* p. 87.

3. *Boston Journal,* June 20, 1870.

4. Frances Harrington, "The Heroine of Lime Rock" *Oceans,* November 1985, pp. 24-27.

5. *Putnam's Magazine,* nd, pp. 521.

6. Both Fisk and Gould were famous "robber barons" of their age.

7. *New York Times,* October 29, 1911.

8. Elizabeth Abbot, "Ida Lewis," [http://www.projo.com/special/women/94root9.htm], January 20, 1999; *Annual Report of the Commissioner of Lighthouses,* various years; *Annual Report of the U.S. Life Saving Service,* 1881, p. 81; George D. Brewerton, *Ida Lewis, The Heroine of Lime Rock,* 1869; Mary Louise Clifford and Candace Clifford, *Women Who Kept the Lights,* (Williamsburg, VA: Cypress Communications, 1993), pp. 91-93; "Clipping File," RG-26, NARA; "Grace Darling Story" [http://www.bandol.u-net.com/grace.htm], August 15, 1999; *Harper's Weekly,* July 31, 1869; "Ida Lewis," [http://www.providenceri.com/narragansettbay/ida_lewis.html], January 20, 1999; "idawally Zorada Lewis," [http://www3.edgenet.net/redwood/notables/IDA_LEWIS.htm], January 20, 1999; *Lighthouse Service Bulletin,* February 1, 1933; *New York Times,* October 22, 25, 26, 29, November 2, 1911; Edward R. Snow, *Famous New England Lighthouses* (Boston: Yankee Publishing, 1945), pp. 436-446; Elizabeth West, "Fifty Years at Lime Rock," *Cobblestone,* June 1981, pp. 10-15;

IV

Kate Walker
The Grand Lightkeeper Of The East Coast

If James Rankin was the grand old lightkeeper of the West Coast, then Kate Walker certainly completes for the same title in the East. Kate kept the important light at Robbins Reef in New York Harbor for 33 years. During this time she was credited with saving 50 persons from drowning.

The first light at Robbins Reef was built in 1839 to help guide ships past a rock ridge and through Ambrose Channel. The nearest land is Staten Island about two and a half miles distant. Robbins Reef was the most isolated of all the lights on the New York approach. The Lighthouse Board replaced the old stone tower with a four-tiered conical iron light in 1883. It was 56 feet high and used a fourth order Fresnel lens with a range of a dozen miles.

For an offshore light, quarters were reasonably comfortable, although everything was circular. The galley and mess room were on the main deck and two bedrooms on the deck above. A visitor remembered the sidewalls and ceiling were cement, painted white and the floors scrubbed to an immaculate cleanliness. Tiny windows were cut into the thick walls. Davits on the outside gallery held the keeper's boat and a 30-foot vertical ladder from the gallery to the water provided access to the light. After Kate moved in the windows were hung with curtains and some of the deeper ledges were given pots of scarlet geraniums.

How Kate came to be keeper is a tale unto itself. The first keeper of the new 1883 light was John Walker. Before his appointment, he was the assistant keeper at Sandy Hook Light in New Jersey. Sandy Hook was located just

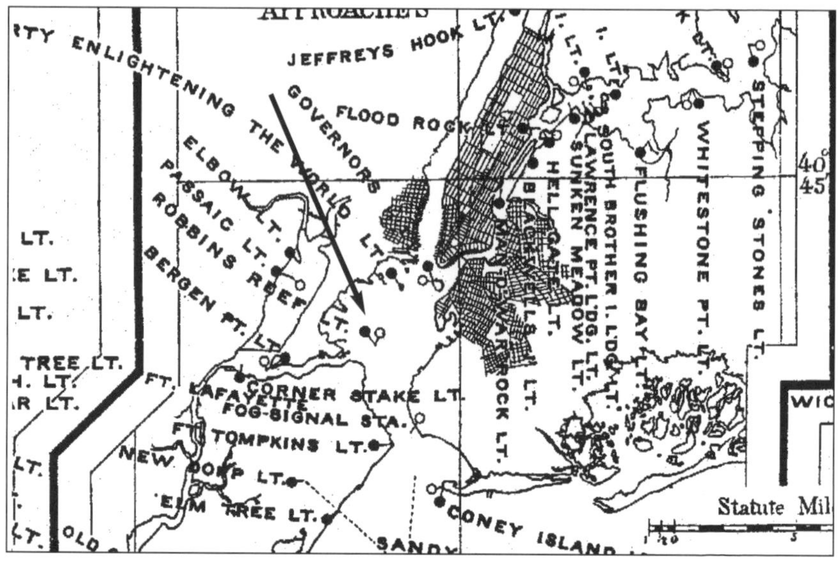

across the bay from New York City. A bachelor, he had been taking his meals at a nearby boarding house where he met a young German immigrant woman who was one of the cooks. It is said the young men of Sandy Hook were in "hot pursuit" of Kate, enchanted by her "sprightliness and good looks." She only spoke German and had a child, but they were not barriers for John. In short order he taught her English, married her and took her to the light at Sandy Hook. In his spare time, he also instructed her how to tend the light.

Kate's lightkeeping knowledge was sufficient that when John was appointed keeper at Robbins Reef at an annual salary of $600, she was appointed assistant keeper at $350. Although doubtlessly pleased at the appointment and the additional income to the family, she was appalled at Robbins Reef. She later said, "When I first came to Robbins Reef, the sight of water, which was ever way I looked, made me lonesome. I refused to unpack my trunks at first, but gradually, a little at a time, I unpacked."[1] At Sandy Hook she had her garden and chickens. Robbins Reef had only water, water, water!

In 1886, John came down with pneumonia and was taken to the hospital. It is said that his last words to his wife as the boat pulled away, were "Mind the light, Kate." And so she did. When her husband died, the District Inspector sent a substitute keeper to allow her to attend John's funeral, but she was back at the light before the day was over. She took comfort in the familiar surroundings of the lighthouse she had come to love.

There was an effort to fill the keeper's position with a man but everyone it was offered to refused it. Perhaps the light was too lonely or perhaps the

Robbins Reef Lighthouse. U.S. Coast Guard photo.

men did not want to deprive Kate of a job. In any case, when Kate applied for the position she was reluctantly given it, and officially appointed by President Benjamin Harrison. There certainly were doubts about her ability to handle it. She was only four feet, 10 inches tall and weighed a mere 100 pounds. Could she stand up to the daily grind of lightkeeping? Many feared for her safety because of the isolation of the station. There were other women keepers, but none were so far from land and so utterly alone!

Her son, Jacob, was appointed as the assistant keeper. Although only 17 years old at the time, family legend claims he was "administratively aged" to 21 to meet the minimum requirement.

Kate proved her doubters wrong. She kept a fine light and rescued a number of people in the course of keeping it. Mostly her victims were fishermen whose craft had blown onto the reef in squalls, but on one occasion a three-masted schooner hit the rocks and rolled on her beam ends. Quickly launching the station boat, she rescued the five crewman plus a small puppy.

Kate gained a certain notoriety around the harbor and it 1906, a reporter for the *New York Times* wrote:

> Mrs. Walker is a stolid, self-possessed, observant woman of the North German type, with shrewd gray eyes, hair that is still untouched by the tint of time, and a complexion as ruddy as a sea captain's. She spends as much time on the terrace outside of her house as she does indoors, even when the wind blows and the salt spray compels her to don an oilskin jacket and a sou'wester. Seen from the decks of passing vessels, this terrace looks as though two goats walking side by side would be crowded. As a matter of fact, three persons walking arm in arm can promenade it very comfortably. In the good old Summer time, when this terrace is sheltered by an awning and dotted with tables and balcony chairs, it is a very inviting place.
>
> Mrs. Walker serves tea there when the bay is smooth enough for her friends to go out in rowboats to see her. In the Winter, when the water is rough and the lighthouse is surrounded with floating ice half the time, Mrs. Walker is virtually a hermit. But in Summer she is as "merry as they make em..." She had a sewing machine and a wind-up phonograph, the latter for the benefit of her son and daughter, who get fidgety once in a while for the sound of a human voice.
>
> All that she knows from personal experience of the great land to which she came as a girl immigrant from Germany is comprised within the limits of Staten Island, New York City and Brooklyn. She says she has never wanted to go West, South or anywhere else. Hours of solitude have taught her, she says, that she is pretty good company when she is

Kate Walker. U.S. Coast Guard photo.

> by herself, and that happiness is being content with the simple things. As a wife, mother and widow, the happiest and saddest days her peaceful life have been spent within the circular walls of her voluntary prison. She declares that if she were compelled to live anywhere else she would be the most miserable woman on earth, and that no mansion on Millionaires' Row could tempt her to leave of her own free will.[2]

The reporter may have romanticized Kate's job somewhat. She was also a mother and a housekeeper, not just a lightkeeper. Every weekday she took Jacob and Mamie, the daughter she had with John, to school in the morning in a rowboat and brought them home in the afternoon.

This meant she had to lower and raise the heavy boat several times a day. It was backbreaking labor at the winch, but she did it day after day, year after year.

After Jacob married, he spent much of his time ashore, taking care of the mail, shopping and other tasks. Doubtlessly, Jacob and his wife would have made the light a very uncomfortable place to live for all.

Kate once said, "This lamp in the tower, it is more difficult to care for than a family of children. It need not be wound more than once in five hours, but I wind it every three hours so as to take no chances. In 19 years that light has never disappointed sailors who depended upon it. Every night I watch it until 12 o'clock. Then, if all is well, I go to bed, leaving my assistant in charge."

The foghorn for Robbins Reef was extremely loud. It was located in the same building Kate lived, and made any attempt to sleep useless. All she could do was stay awake until the fog cleared. Should the siren break, a large bell was on the roof. Kate had to climb up and ring it by hand until either the fog cleared or someone repaired the siren.

Kate and her family sometimes found themselves in the middle of strange situations, as this account illustrated:

> It is a very swift and treacherous tide around there at times, fully as bad as at Hell Gate. A young man who took his sweetheart out in a rowboat from New Brighton one Summer Sunday afternoon did not heed the warning given to him. The tide carried him squarely onto the rocks around the lighthouse. His boat had a hole in her bow and was almost full of water when he assisted his companion up the iron ladder and let her have her cry out, while he conferred with the keeper. She dried their clothes while they sat out in the sun in decidedly castaway costume. Jake [Jacob] was ashore as night came on. He might not be back before morning. The girl was in despair.
>
> "We shall miss the last train to Fishkill," she exclaimed, and "I shall have to remain in town all night. Oh, what will they think of me?"
>
> "See here," said the young man, "You say the word and we'll get married on Staten Island tonight and send them a telegram explaining all about it."
>
> The girl was at first indignant, then reluctant, but finally consented. But how to get ashore? As luck would have it, one of Mamie's friends rowed out to the lighthouse that evening to pay a call. He entered into the spirit of the thing. The castaways were taken ashore, married by a minister at the close of evening service, and started off on a happy honeymoon.[3]

Kate was a fixture in the New York maritime scene. Captains often called Robbins Reef "Kate's Light." It was said she could identify the different vessels passing the light by the sound of their whistles. On one occasion, she and a friend were walking in Manhattan when she heard a noon whistle blow. She said, "That sounds like the *Richard B. Morse's* whistle, but the *Morse* was scrapped years ago." It turned out it was the same whistle, bought secondhand from the ship breaker's by the factory!

A reporter once asked Kate about the people she saved. "Generally they joke and laugh about it. I've never made my mind up whether they are courageous or stupid. Maybe they don't know how near they have come to their Maker, or perhaps they know and are not afraid. But I think that in the adventure they haven't realized how near their souls have been to taking flight from the body."

One special incident was the wreck of a schooner which struck the reef. Kate launched her dinghy and took aboard the five crewman as well as a small Scottie dog, whose survival pleased her greatly. At the end of her career, Kate remembered, "He crouched, shivering, against my ankles. I'll never forget the look in his big brown eyes as he raised them to mine." Reaching the lighthouse, she carried him inside her cloak to the kitchen, where she put the dog on the floor. It promptly fell over as if it were dead. Reaching to the stove, Kate poured out some coffee from the pot she always kept hot in the stormy weather and poured some of the dark liquid down the dog's throat. "Then his eyes opened, and there was that same thankful look he had given me in the boat." A week later the captain returned and took back the dog. As he was being carried down the lighthouse ladder, the Scottie looked up and whined. "It was then I realized that dogs really weep, for there were tears in Scottie's eyes. It is strange that one of the most pleasant memories I have of my more than 30 years in the lighthouse should be of the loving gratitude of a dog."

Kate retired in 1919, moving to nearby Tompkinville, New York. Her son, Jacob, replaced her as keeper but only stayed on for two years before resigning to become a painting contractor. She died at age 83 on February 5, 1931. Her obituary in the *New York Evening Post* in part noted, "A great city's waterfront is rich in romance …there are queenly liners, the grim battle craft, the countless carriers of commerce that pass in endless procession. And amid all this and in sight of the city of towers and the torch of liberty lived this sturdy little woman, proud of her work and content in it, keeping her lamp alight and her windows clean, so that New York might be safe for ships that pass in the night."[4]

Upon her death, a local poet, David B. Hermann, wrote a tribute to her life. Although he uses fictitious names, he stated it was intended as a tribute to Kate.

The wind was roaring o'er the sea,
The waves in fury lashed,
The rocks around the lighthouse base,
The thunder rolled and crashed.

The atramentous blackness,
Of the seething, frenzied night,
Was pierced by the lightning,
And the beacon's brilliant light.

The bright unfailing beacon,
That pointed ceaselessly,
With its yellow finger,
Down the highways of the sea.

To light the ships upon their way,
And cheer each sailor's soul,
To keep the snarling, hungry reef,
From taking human toll.

Inside the rounded lighthouse walls,
Shut in from the night,
Lay in a room, upon a cot,
The keeper of the light.

His face was haggard, pale and drawn;
The only sign he gave of life,
Was the movement of his lips,
As he whispered to his wife.

Who by his bedside sadly sat,
Smoothing down his ruffled hair,
On her face the lines of grief,
And in her heart, despair.

"Anne," the lighthouse keeper said,
"I feel right strange tonight,
But then, I am a dying man –
Annie, burns the light?

"You're not crying, are you, Annie?
Or is it the wind I hear,
Blowing round the lighthouse top?
No, that sobbing is too near.

"Do not feel so bad darling,
Every man must die, you know;
I'll meet you up in Heaven, Annie,
Only for a while I go.

"And the short time we are parted,
Faithfully, night after night,
For the ships and for your Ned,
Darling Annie, keep the light."

Suddenly his lips ceased moving,
Soon he lay as still as death;
Annie, terror in her eyes,
Watched his grasping for his breath.

She clasped him in her arms and cried,
"Ned! Speak to me! Ned"
Then uttered a soul-rending sob;
His lips were cold and dead.

She held him tightly in her arms,
Bathed with her tears his cheek,
Madly kissed his heedless lips,
Then sat from sorrow weak.

Every evening, ever after,
When the sun had safely set,
Annie climbed the winding stair,
Her eyes with tears were wet.

Although her Ned had passed away,
His spirit still was there,
It climbed up too the light with Annie,
Helped her mount each stair.

A sailorman who knew her,
Whose ship passed in the night,
Said to a seaman at his side,
"Annie keeps the light."

"She herself is faith and courage,
And as brightly as her love,
She keeps the beacon burning here,
Till she joins her mate above."

By any accounting, Kate was a remarkable woman.[5]

Marinette Marine has really worked hard to make the launching ceremony special, including having actors portray the vessel's namesakes. From left: Kate Walker, Marinette Marine Corporation's President Dan Gulling and Ida Lewis. Marinette Marine Corporation photo.

Footnotes

1. "Clipping File," RG-26, NARA.

2. "Clipping File," RG-26, NARA.

3. *New York Times,* March 5, 1906.

4. *New York Times,* March 5, 1906.

5. Hans Christian Adamson, *Keepers of the Lights* (New York: Greenberg Publisher, 1955), pp. 127-128; *Annual Reports, U.S. Lighthouse Service,* various (Washington, D.C.: Government Printing Office); Mary Louise Clifford and J. Candace Clifford, *Women Who Kept the Lights* (Williamsburg, VA: Cypress Communications, 1993), pp. 127-134; "Clipping File," RG-26, NARA; Dennis Noble, *Lighthouses and Keepers* (Annapolis, Maryland: U.S. Naval Institute Press, 1997), pp. 114-115;

The Katherine Walker *hits the water with a thunderous splash. Marinette Marine Corporation photo.*

V

Abbie Burgess Who Kept The Light Burning

One of the greatest names in lightkeeping history is that of Abbie Burgess. Her story is one of bravery and dedication to duty to the highest degree. Regardless of circumstance, danger or adversity, she always managed to "keep the light burning."

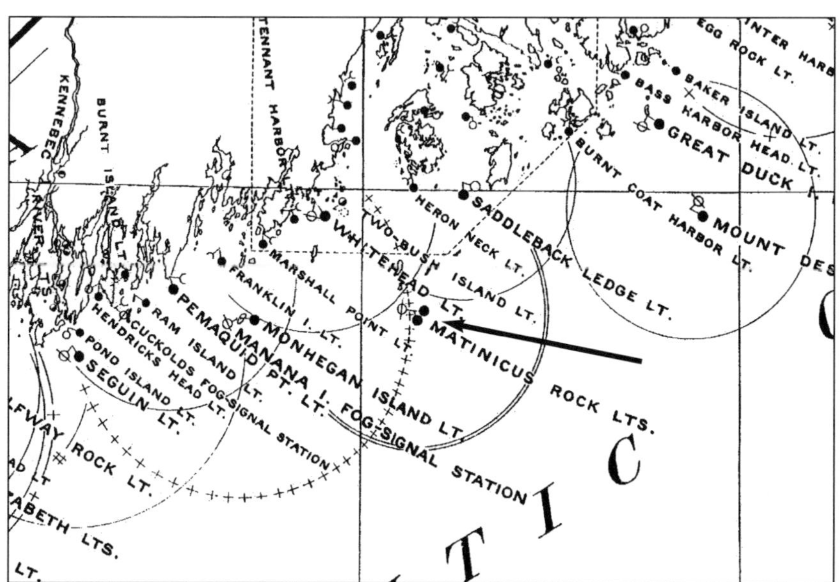

Abbie Burgess. U.S. Coast Guard photo.

Abbie's lightkeeping career started at Matinicus Rock, Maine. She first saw the bleak and desolate island in 1853 when she was barely 14 years old. It sits 22 miles off the entrance of Penobscot Bay, Maine. No trees or grass grew on the forsaken island. When the big storms rolled in from the wide Atlantic, waves were known to wash completely over the island. One bored keeper measured the island as 2,350 feet long and 567 feet wide. The nearest populated land is Matinicus Island, six miles distant and the closest town of any consequence was Rockland, Maine, 25 miles away. It is known as the most isolated light along the Maine coast.

The first lighthouse was built at Matinicus Rock in 1826. Made cheaply of wood, it consisted of a keeper's house with a tower at each end. It lasted

Matinicus Rock was a bleak outpost, photo circa 1940s. U.S. Coast Guard photo.

for 20 years, a short life for a lighthouse. A new stone structure was build, but it held up for a mere decade before being replaced with a cut stone towers. The history of Matinicus Light is replete with rebuilding and repairing the buildings and towers. It truly was man standing against the ravages of nature.

In April 1853, Abbie's father, Samuel Burgess, was appointed keeper at an annual salary of $450. He soon moved to the island with his invalid wife, Thankful, four daughters and two sons. The elder boy, Benjamin, known to the family as "Benji", soon left home to become a fisherman, leaving Abbie as the oldest to be her father's assistant. Three older daughters were already living elsewhere.

Under his expert guidance, she learned the ins and outs of the lightkeeper's job. This was no mere intellectual exercise on Abbie's part. He father was not always at the lighthouse. In his spare time he went lobstering and when he went ashore to sell his catch, Abbie was left in charge not only of the other children, but also the light. Abbie was a very busy girl. Each tower had 14 Argland lamps to be lit at dark, checked frequently throughout the night and cleaned and made ready again in the morning. It is said that by the time she was 17, she was really the lightkeeper, in fact if not by official appointment. Local sailors knew all about Abbie of Matinicus.

Abbie also kept chickens on the island. While they were very important as a source of fresh eggs, they also grew to be pets to her. Once, she even rescued them from imminent destruction.

In January 1856, Abbie's father went to the mainland to buy supplies. The regular supply cutter had not made it to he island and it was important to restock the family larder before winter set in. The lateness of the season and the likelihood his return would be delayed bothered Burgess. It is said that just before he rowed away he told his daughter, "I can depend on you, Abbie." Shortly after he left, the wind veered to the northeast and began to blow. For three days the storm built in intensity. On the morning of the fourth day, a wave surged over the island and smashed into the keeper's house. When it was obvious they were in for a bad storm, Abbie had moved the family into one of the stone towers which were far stronger than the building. Watching the grey seas lash the house, she was glad he had moved everyone!

Abbie later wrote:

> The new dwelling was flooded and the windows had to be secured to prevent the violence of the spray from breaking them in. As the tide came, the sea rose higher and higher, till the only endurable places were the light-towers. If they stood, we were saved, otherwise our fate was only too certain. But for some reason, I know not why, I had no

Abbie and the chickens. U.S. Coast Guard collection.

misgivings, and went on with my work as usual. For four weeks, owing to rough weather, no landing could be effected on the Rock. During this time we were without the assistance of any male member of our family. Though at times greatly exhausted with my labors, not once did the lights fail. Under God I was able to perform all of my accustomed duties as well as my father's.

You know the hens were our only companions. Becoming convinced, as the gale increased, that unless they were brought into the house they would be lost, I said to mother: "I must try to save them." She advised me not to attempt it. The thought, of parting with them without and effort was not to be endured, so seizing a basket, I ran out a few yards after the rollers had passed and the sea fell off a little, with the water knee deep, to the coop, and rescued all but one. It was the work of a moment, and I was back in the house with the door fastened,

> but I was none too quick, for at that instant, my little sister, standing at the window, exclaimed: "Oh, look! look There! the worst sea is coming!
>
> That wave destroyed the old dwelling and swept the Rock ...The sea is never still, and when agitated, its roar shuts out every other sound, even drowning our voices.

Several days later her father returned safely. Abbie was praised many times over for her bravery in manning the light. Perhaps in recognition that male help was needed, on August 19, 1856, Abbie's brother Benji was appointed assistant keeper at an annual salary of $300, serving until the end of his father's term.

The following year Abbie was again left on the Rock while her father went to Rockland for supplies. This time her brother Benji was with her. Again a vicious storm roared into the island. When there was a lull in the northeast blasts, Benji left in a small boat for stores. He soon disappeared amid the rolling grey seas. For the next 21 days Abbie and her charges waited for their return. As day followed day, they could only believe both perished in the storm. Food was so short the family was reduced to a daily allowance of an egg and cup of corn meal mush! Finally, both Benji and his father returned with boatloads of food.

Life at the Rock was nothing if not lonely for Abbie. As a young girl growing into womanhood, she was 25 miles from any social activity. Church socials, barn dances or Sunday visiting, were all activities she could only dream about. She had no girlfriends or real opportunities to have eligible young men "come a-spark'n."

During this time, the appointment of lightkeepers was very much a political process. When Abraham Lincoln was elected in 1860, Burgess was out of a job. On March 29, 1861, Captain John Grant was appointed in his place. Abbie remained at Matinicus to show the new keeper how the lamps and other apparatus worked. During her stay she worked closely with Grant's son, Isaac, who was appointed assistant keeper. On September 7, 1861, 26-year-old Isaac and 22-year-old Abbie were married. Soon after, Abbie was also officially appointed as an assistant keeper with her husband. Life on the lonely Rock agreed with the newlyweds, and before they left Matinicus their family had grown to four children.

Abbie was apparently not Isaac's first wife. On October 16, 1854, it was reported he married Amanda M. Thompson. There was one child who died at an early age. What happened to Amanda isn't known.

Abbie's father-in-law, Captain John Grant, had a remarkable career as a lightkeeper. He remained as the Matinicus keeper until June 21, 1867, when he was replaced by Christopher Chase. However, Grant remained at

Matinicus as the assistant keeper until he was reinstated as keeper on March 22, 1871, a position he held until 1890. His whole family assisted in the enterprise. Sons, Isaac, John and William, daughter Mary, son-in-law Knott C. Perry, and daughter-in-law Abbie, all helped keep the light at various times. When he finally retired he was 85 years old!

In 1875, Isaac was appointed keeper at Whitehead Light 20 miles distant, so Abbie and her family departed the Rock for their new home. His appointment was announced in the *Rockland Gazette* on May 20, 1875: "Capt. Isaac H. Grant, late 1st assistant lightkeeper at Matinicus Rock, took charge of the Whitehead Light Station last Saturday, as principal keeper, to which position he was appointed upon the resignation of the late very efficient keeper, Mr. Hezekiah Long. Capt. Grant is a thoroughly reliable man, who will deserve any trust confided in him, and we congratulate him on his promotion. His wife is appointed assistant. At Mantinicus, Wm. Grant, former 2nd assistant, has been promoted to first assistant. Mr. John F. Grant has been appointed 2nd assistant and Miss Mary B. Grant 3rd assistant."[1]

Abbie's husband was a brave man. On August 7, 1881, he took the lead in a daring rescue of two sailors from the schooner *Vicksburg*, an act that resulted in his being awarded the Silver Life Saving Service medal. The official recommendation from the Life Saving keeper speaks eloquently not only of Isaac's courage, but also the involvement of the whole family:

> While filling up the report of the capsized yawl boat, disaster to which occurred August 7th, near While Head Island, I have felt it my

Left: Abbie's gravestone. Right: a small lighthouse adorns her grave. U.S. Coast Guard photos.

duty to inform you of the heroic conduct, on that occasion, of Capt. Isaac H. Grant Keeper of White Head Light. It has been Capt. Grant's habit whenever a "scale" or "clear up" of the fog has occurred to go out and look around to see if any vessels have got ashore…. On the present occasion, the fog suddenly clearing up, he discovered the two men clinging to the bottom of the boat and acted with his usual characteristic promptness and energy. He hurried off to the rescue taking his own boat (the nearest boat to the scene of the disaster), his son Frank Grant going with him. At the same time he sent his little daughter Miss Mary L. Grant to notify me of the accident. The little girl ran all the way and on reaching her destination, could speak only in a whisper. On reaching the vicinity of the South Breaker Capt. Grant was forced to throw away his iron ballast and his sail to keep his boat from swamping. His boat being [a] heavy sail boat and ballasted was poorly fitted to go into so rough and heavy seas. In this trip he passed over a dangerous shoal that lay in the way to the yawl. It was so rough that a boat could be seen but a short distance away and he had not seen our boat till he had taken the

Abbie Burgess *underway on trials. Marinette Marine Corporation photo.*

The tender Abbie Burgess *follows in the tradition of the famous lightkeeper. Marinette Marine Corporation photo.*

> men off the yawl and we were nearly along side of his boat.... Our boat took the rescued men to the Light House that being the nearest house. Here Capt. Grant's family did every thing in their power to make them comfortable, his wife tearing up sheets for bandages. Captain Grant furnished them with dry clothes, coffee and dinner.[2]

Abbie and Isaac continued at Whitehead until March 31, 1890, when they both resigned from the Lighthouse Service. In May of that year they moved to Middlesborough, Massachusetts, likely influenced by her sister Ester, who had moved there two years prior. The Lighthouse Service must have been in their blood however, because within two years the family was living in Portland, Maine, and Isaac was employed as the keeper of the U.S. Lamphouse. He remained in charge of the store house until 1910.

Abbie Burgess died at South Portland on June 16, 1892, at age 53 and was buried at Forest Hill Cemetery in South Thomaston, near the town of Spruce Head, near the Whitehead Light. Her husband was also buried there upon his death in 1918.

Abbie was always a letter writer and in one of her last, she wrote, "I think the time is not too far distant when I shall climb these lighthouse stairs no more.... I wonder if the care of the lighthouse will follow my soul after it has left this worn-out body! If I ever have a gravestone, I would like it in the form of a lighthouse or beacon." Fifty-seven years after her death, New England maritime historian Edward R.Snow saw to it that her wish was granted, and a little lighthouse-shaped stone was placed on her grave.[3]

Footnotes

1. *Rockland Gazette* (Rockland, Maine), May 20, 1875.

2. RG 26, NARA.

3. Hans Christian Adamson, *Keepers of the Lights,* (New York: Greenberg, 1955), pp. 78-81; *Annual Reports, U.S. Lighthouse Service,* various years; Mary Louise Clifford and J. Candace Clifford, *Women Who Kept the Lights* (Williamsburg, VA: Cypress Communications, 1993), pp. 23-29; "Clipping File," RG-26, NARA; Mary Johns, "Abbie Burgess Launched," [http://www.1hdigest.com/archives/1887/may97/Burgess.htm], February 3, 1999; *New England Historical and Genealogical Register,* Volume 152, October 1998, pp. 391-417; Edward R. Snow, *Famous New England Lighthouses* (Boston: Yankee Publishing Co., 1945), pp. 27-41.

VI
James Rankin of Fort Point Light

One of the longest-serving West Coast keepers was James Rankin. He was born in Killshee County, Ireland, in 1844, and immigrated to the United States from Liverpool, England, in 1867. Ireland, beset by periodic famine and plight, was no place for an ambitious man. After naturalization, he joined the U.S. Coast and Geodetic Survey as a "leading man," or in more common terms, "leading seaman." He spent 10 years sailing aboard the Survey's vessel *U.S.S. Hassler*.

Apparently desiring a career change, he joined the Lighthouse Service in 1877, and was assigned to the East Brother Light in San Pablo Bay, just to the north of San Francisco.

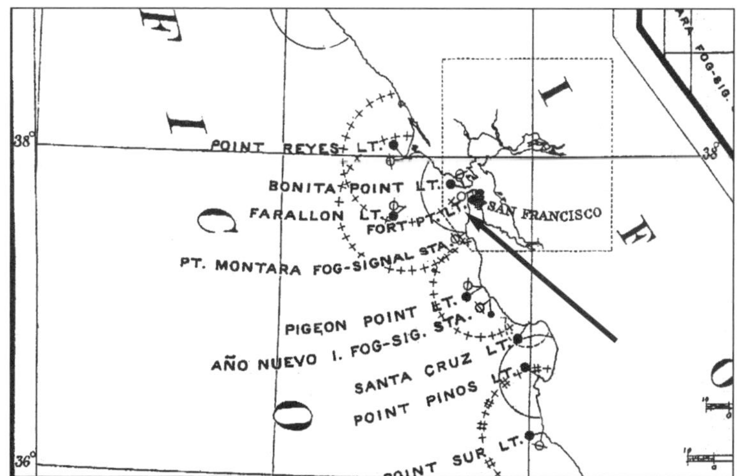

James Rankin. U.S. Coast Guard photo.

He transferred to the Fort Point Light on August 20 of the following year. Fort Point Light is near the famous Presidio at San Francisco. Fort Point was also the site of California's second lighthouse, the first being at Alcatraz in 1852. The first Fort Point Light, barely three months old, was torn down when the Army decided to erect Fort Winfield Scott on the site to protect San Francisco.

The second light was built on a narrow ledge between the fort and sea wall. It was finished in 1855. The location, however, was not a good one. The sea wall began eroding which in turn undercut the lighthouse and eventually required building a new light.

The third light was actually built on top of the stone bastions of the fort, giving it a height of 83 feet above the sea. The iron skeleton tower was a bare 27 feet high. The watch room was entered by climbing an exposed circular stairway and then ducking through a small iron scuttle hatch. Inside the watch room the furnishing were Spartan, a table for trimming wicks and performing minor equipment maintenance, stand for a five gallon oil drum, lamp and lens cleaning supplies, linen aprons, a clock and other similar items. The lens was a fourth order Fresnel.

Fort Point Light, amid the cannons. The dangerous bridge is in the foreground. U.S. Coast Guard photo.

Fort Point also had a unique fog signal. The massive, 3,000-pound bell was mounted on a platform jutting out from the bastion wall over the water. A clockwork mechanism sounded it as required. To reach the bell to activate it, the keeper had to make his way carefully down a narrow ladder mounted on the wall. Rankin and his assistants literally risked their lives to service the signal. The bell was located just under the mouths of the cannon and, by 1869, had become quite battered by the heavy concussion of cannon fire. In 1904, it was replaced with a compressed air foghorn located in a building adjacent to the tower. In 1911, the horns were replaced with a siren. The bell, however, remained for emergency use.

Keeper's house, Fort Point. U.S. Coast Guard photo.

Rankin at rest. U.S. Coast Guard photo.

Rankin remained as the keeper for the next 41 years. He and his family lived in the small keeper's house located on a bluff just south of the fort. Dwellings for the assistant keepers were nearby. Old records talk about how dangerous it was to go down the bluff and cross the windy gap to the fort. The bluff and fort formed a kind of funnel and when a storm was blowing, the wind tore through with an unholy force. To provide a safer route, a foot bridge was built from the bluff to the fort. In high winds however, Rankin and his men were afraid they would be swept off the bridge and used the lower route. The wind was so powerful the Lighthouse Service actually had to cable the keeper's houses to the ground to prevent their being blown away! Over the years his three children and eight grandchildren would be born at Fort Point. It was the only home they knew.

It has been said that Rankin was the last of the West Coast's "grand old lightkeepers." Not only did he keep the light burning, but he was an active

The keeper and his family. U.S. Coast Guard photo.

lifesaver, always willing to try to save those in peril in the dangerous waters off his station. Fort Point was located in an especially hazardous location. As the tide rushes into the bay, it veers sharply toward Fort Point where the sea slams violently into the sea wall. Its foaming ferocity can propel a swimmer across the sharp rocks and crush him against the stone wall. Powerful undertow can pull the victim, dead or still alive, back into the depths of the sea.

The nearby U.S. Life Saving Station usually posted a lookout at the point, to keep watch for vessels in trouble. To help pass the time, the lookout often practiced knot-tying using his lifeline:

> At the conclusion of one of these sessions, a crewman heard shouts and saw that a person was drowning. He grabbed his rope and raced to the sea wall, seeing a boy foundering off shore. Preparing to toss the boy a line, he looked at the hopelessly knotted mass in his hand and realized that the rope was useless.
>
> Rankin's arrival prevented this moment from becoming a tragedy. Carrying a ladder in one hand and a life preserver in the other, Rankin put the ladder over the side and climbed down to the sea wall. Using the life preserver to stay afloat, he swam out and brought the boy to safety.

The youth recovered enough to say that his father was somewhere clinging to an overturned boat. The lifesaving crew, having responded to a phone call, arrived in time to save the father.

Even on land you faced the possibility of danger at Fort Point. Two couples were out picnicking one Sunday afternoon. After several bottles of wine, they began playing a portable Victrola and dancing. After a time one couple decided that the sea wall was a much more exciting place to dance and it was. The two dancers shortly lost their footing and fell into the bay. A fisherman saw the couple, already being swept out to sea on the ebb tide and ran to Keeper Rankin's house, raising the alarm. Rankin and his son grabbed their favorite lifesaving tools, the ladder and life preserver and headed for the sea wall.

Assistant keeper Kunder and Rankin's son in law August Nagel, also went into action, giving a performance reminiscent of a Keystone Cops comedy. Knowing the gravity of the situation, they searched frantically for a rope. Finally, unable to find a rope the assistant keeper yelled to Nagel to grab the garden hose and run for the sea wall. Nagel did just that, forgetting that the other end was still attached to the faucet. This rescue ended shortly after Nagel reached the garden gate, as the hose stretched taut and all forward progress ceased. Kunder and Nagel went back and unscrewed the hose and again started for the beach. When they arrived it was all over. The disheveled dancers were being helped up the ladder by the keeper and his son. The lady's full skirt acted like a parachute and trapped a great deal of air, keeping her afloat. The husband, not having the same advantage, had been forced to swim for it. In order to save the couple, Rankin had found it necessary to strip. When the Victorian lady saw Rankin naked, she became hysterical, screaming, "I've never seen a naked man in my life except my husband."

One of the other picnickers was still running around the fort yelling, "Get a rope! Get a rope!" The exhausted keeper found himself standing by the sea wall, naked, with a distraught women yelling and pointing at him, and a man continuing to circle the fort shouting for a rope for a rescue already completed. It was almost enough to make a man consider another line of work!

Fort Point has experienced some tremendous storms. During one blow in 1888, the heavy storm-shutters were wrenched off the keepers house, breaking the windows and forcing the families to shelter in protected rooms to wait out the violence. During the night, Rankin and his assistants had to tend the light and thus left their families in the house. The wind was so strong the men had to crawl on hands and knees to reach the fort and the tower. Climbing the exterior stairway to the watch room was very dangerous. They went hand-over-hand up the iron stairs, grabbing firmly to the handrails. It seemed that every moment the grasping wind was about to blow them off. Inside the watch room they discovered the force of the winds was actually making the tower sway! Throughout the long stormy night the men stayed in the rocking tower, doubtlessly wondering if the next blast of wind would blow the tower over. In spite of the light, a ship, thought to be the *City of Chester*, sank off the point.

On June 15, 1913, Rankin swam to the rescue of a man from an over-turned boat. The same year he used a rope to aid two men from a capsized rowboat. When he performed these rescues, he was 69 years old!

Even though the Fort Point Light was collocated with the Army garrison, the keepers drew their supplies from the Lighthouse Service. The tender *Madrono* came every six months and it was a long time between her visits. Doubtlessly, Rankin and his family socialized with the men at the fort, helping to east the isolation. Until the keepers built a winch-powered tramway from the wharf to the bluff, all of the lighthouse supplies had to be carried up by hand. Most of the construction work was done by Rankin and his assistants.

The 1906 earthquake that destroyed San Francisco shook Fort Winfield Scott, too, but caused very little damage, other than knocking the chimneys on the keeper's houses over and disturbing the footbridge foundation.

As Rankin grew close to his retirement, local reporters began to pay attention to the grand old lightkeeper. One asked him what there was to see at Fort Point? Rankin replied, "There is nothing to see. There is the ocean and the sand and the guns and the soldiers. That is all. It grows monotonous. Always the ocean and the sand and guns and the soldiers. As for the ships, one grows tired of them, too. I have my family and my pleasures."[1] He also showed reporters some of his paintings–landscapes in oil showing views from Fort Point.

Rankin continued to make regular rescues until the very end of his service days. His last two rescues, those of young boys from the rocks on December 29, 1918, and on January 6, 1919, earned letters of commendation from the Secretary of Commerce. At the time, he was 77 years old! Upon his retirement at age 78 on February 28, 1919, the Commissioner of Lighthouses wrote Rankin, commending him for saving the lives of 18 people during his long career.

Without a lighthouse to keep, Rankin and his wife moved to Antioch, California, where he died on January 5, 1921. He was certainly the last of the old breed of lighthouse men!

The James Rankin *hits the water! Marinette Marine Corporation photo.*

Fort Point Light was discontinued on September 1, 1934, with the erection of the Golden Gate Bridge. The north tower blocked both the light and foghorn from vessels passing through the Golden Gate. Today Fort Point Light is part of the Golden Gate National Recreation Area. The old light itself sits directly under the Golden Gate bridge, dwarfed by the monstrous symbol of automotive progress.[2]

Footnotes

1. Ralph Shanks and Lisa Woo Shanks, editor *Guardians of the Golden Gate, Lighthouses and Lifeboat Stations of San Francisco Bay* (Petaluma, California: Costano Books, 1990), p.117.

2. *Annual Report of the Commissioner of Lighthouses, 1913*, (Washington, DC: Government Printing Office, 1913); "Clipping File," RG-26, NARA; "Lighthouse Service Bulletin," July, 1913, pp. 74-75, December, 1934; "Naming File," U.S. Coast Guard Historian's Office; Shanks, *Guardians*, pp. 105-127.

VII
Frank Drew To The Rescue Again!

Frank Drew was probably the most prolific lifesaving lighthouse keeper on the Great Lakes. Time and again, when people were in trouble near his light, he was quick to the rescue.

Frank was born on Green Island, Wisconsin, on March 11, 1864, and began his lightkeeping career at Lake Michigan's Pilot Island, at the entrance to Green Bay, as an acting second assistant keeper on January 10, 1899. Pilot Island was also known as "Port du Morts" Light. He served in that capacity

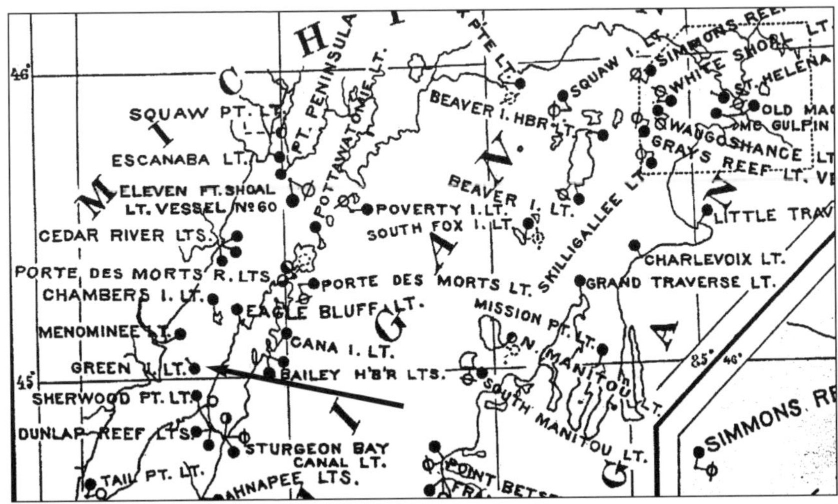

Frank Drew. U.S. Coast Guard photo.

until April 1, 1900, when he was promoted to first assistant. He remained at Pilot Island until October 31, 1903, when transferred out to Green Island Light as first assistant. He was appointed keeper on July 15, 1909, and remained there until his retirement on April 1, 1929.

Green Island is located in the bay of Green Bay and is four miles from the mouth of the Menominee River. It is roughly 87 acres. At the time the light was established in 1863, it was a wooded island roughly three-quarters of a mile long. A reef extends west from the northwest end for a mile, and a half-mile-long sand spit extends southeast from the southeast end. The shoals can shift due to ice action. As the result of extensive sand and gravel dredging near the island, the entire area is considered fouled and large draft vessels should stand clear.

Green Island Light was first exhibited on October 1, 1863. The tower was wood, painted white, and placed on top of the keeper's house. A fourth order Fresnel lens showed a fixed white light visible for 12 nautical miles.

Green Island Light circa 1904. U.S. Coast Guard photo.

Green Island Light. U.S. Coast Guard photo.

The first keeper was Samuel P. Drew, appointed on October 26, 1863. His wife was appointed assistant keeper. There are two stories as to how he came to be keeper. In the first he was a lighthouse keeper on Chambers Island (prior to 1863) and was transporting a government inspector to Beaver Island when the inspector told him of the government's intention. The inspector added that within a few days he would purchase the island (Green Island) on behalf of the government. "Drew delivered his passenger to Beaver Island, then hurried to the mainland to purchase Green Island from the Indians ahead of the government for $500. A few days later he sold the government 17 acres of the island for the same amount with the provision that he hold the lighthouse keeper's position there." A second story says that he tried to enlist in the Army but was too short and became a shoemaker instead. He made a fine pair of boots for a man who was unable to pay and in settlement, he received the island. He was previously a keeper at nearby Rock Island.

Green Island Light may have been the first lighthouse to try mineral oil, also called kerosene, as a fuel instead of the stipulated whale oil. Records only show that "...in 1864, a Lake Michigan lightkeeper on his own responsibility used a kerosene lamp in his light, but after several nights an explosion scattered oil all over the keeper and a second violent explosion blew the whole lantern from the tower and destroyed the lens."[1] The same year the

Green Island Lighthouse suffered fire damage and a temporary tower was constructed. While the evidence is only circumstantial, none the less it is tantalizing to assume it was Green Island Light.

Regardless of how Samuel Drew came to be appointed lightkeeper, by 1867 he owned half the island. He built several buildings on his land, including a home and a private dock and boathouse. Besides keeping the light, Samuel Drew also farmed on the island, raising strawberries, corn, wheat, potatoes and oats which the family sold in Menekaunee, east of Marinette, Wisconsin.

Sam and his wife, Mary, had seven children. Three, including Frank, were born on Green Island. A sister, Anna, died in the fall of 1869, when she was less than three months old, and is buried on the island. Stormy weather prevented Sam from getting her to the mainland for medical treatment. Her grave was once marked with a tombstone, which vandals later stole. In a happier theme, two of Frank's sisters, Helen and Mary, were married on the island. Perhaps desiring a more metropolitan setting, on May 27, 1881, Samuel Drew transferred to the Menominee Pierhead Light. His duty there was short. On August 31, 1882, he died.

An old newspaper story about Frank Drew's life stated that "The first thing he remembers vividly is the wrecking of the three-masted schooner *George L. Newman*. It was 9 P.M. on Oct. 8, 1871, the night of the great Chicago fire, when the *Newman* stranded on a reef off the island. There were other fires that night and the smoke from a forest fire near Pestigo was so dense that the captain of the schooner could not see the beacon. Embers rained over the island. The crew was saved and stayed on the island for a week salvaging what they could." Frank was only seven years old at the time.[2]

Eighteen eighty-two was an important year for Frank. Both of his parents died and he became a sailor. His first trip away from Green Island ended in a very abrupt fashion. He was employed as a cook on the three-masted schooner *Veto* and when the ship reached Chicago, he was fired. It seems the master became enamored of a young girl and took her aboard as cook. Drew had to go to make room for his captain's dalliance.

For the next 17 years, Drew worked on tugs, fishing boats, lumber hookers and schooners. He quickly climbed the ladder of rank, too. When the *Lady Washington* grounded in a gale near Manistique, Michigan, he was her mate. At the young age of 25 he was the captain of a passenger and package steamer and earning a good salary. Two years later he married Mary Louisa Mayville in Point St. Ignace, Michigan.

Perhaps in an effort to achieve some stability in his life, in 1899, he left the lakes and entered the Lighthouse Service. His first assignment was at Pilot Island, at the tip Lake Michigan's Door Peninsula, and just 13 miles from where his father was keeper at Rock Island. Tragedy struck in 1902 when his wife died. By then he had three young children and wanted to raise them closer to relatives, so he arranged a transfer to Green Island as first assistant keeper to James Wachter. Just getting to Green Island from Pilot Island nearly proved the end of the family. It took them 17 days to battle their way over the 49 mile distance in his small schooner, fighting ice and winds all the way. Six years later, Frank became keeper at Green Island and remained so for 20 years until he retired.

Repairs and changes to light stations were common and it was no different during Frank's tenure. In 1903, the boat landings were almost completely destroyed by ice during the winter, requiring repair. In 1906, new landing cribs were built and placed and a new boat house and boatways were added, including a winch and car.

Green Island saw its share of shipwrecks. On October 26, 1903, shortly before Frank arrived at the station, the steamer *Erie L. Hackley* sank off the

Frank Drew and family, circa 1913. U.S. Coast Guard photo.

eastern shore of the island. Eight passengers and three crewman including the captain, were lost. Several survivors spent over 14 hours floating on wreckage before they were rescued by the steamer *Sheboygan*. Years later, while a ship was dredging gravel off the south side of the island, a woman's shoes came up with bones still in them. They were believed to be from one of the passengers on the steamer.

Frank solved one of the lightkeeper's traditional problems, that of keeping the light under constant observation. He thought the problem over and solved it by erecting a mirror on the lawn, where he could watch the light from the comfort of the keeper's house. It is also thought he planted 44 apple trees in the center of the island. As late as 1992, they we still producing apples.

In the 1920s when Frank was keeper, the light was remembered:

> On the government portion was the main dwelling, a lovely brick building with a tower and a light. Four rooms on the first floor, one of which was used as an office and a also a large entry way with stairway upstairs which also had four rooms plus hallway to another set of stairs leading up to the tower. All the rooms and hallways had hardwood floors. In the back of the brick building a kitchen had been added with a pantry (in the pantry was a trap door in the floor which opened onto steps leading to a cellar for keeping food cool). Attached to the kitchen was a wing jutting south which was divided into a large entry way and a room for washing clothes.
>
> The woodwork in the main building was all white, the kitchen was a pale grey (which when water was dropped on it turned white). All the doorknobs were brass and had to be polished quite frequently.
>
> Also on the government portion was a boathouse near a dock, a shed and workshop - whitewashed instead of painted. A small building of brick called an oil house, I believe they kept kerosene there and along side of it was a huge tank which was for gasoline.
>
> Log books were kept in the office, weather conditions recorded, what time the light was lit, how it performed during the night and what time it was extinguished in the morning, and many other items of interest.
>
> Finger marks were cleaned off woodwork daily, the brass was polished weekly, the light in the tower was cleaned daily.[3]

Nineteen thirty-three was the last year Green Island was manned. Thereafter it was an automated station, on at dusk and off at dawn, without the firm hand of a human keeper. In 1956-57, the light proper was moved to

Green Island Lighthouse today. Vandals destroyed what storms could not. Marinette Marine Corporation photo.

a 60-foot tower. The Roen Steamship Company purchased the island in 1955, and the lighthouse and other structures in 1957. They attempted to mine the island for gravel, but the government stopped them for environmental reasons. Time, fire and vandals have since destroyed the lighthouse.

Drew received many mentions and commendations in both the *Annual Report of the Commissioner of Lighthouses* and *Lighthouse Service Bulletin*. All of his rescues were made while he was at Green Island.

•1912–Commended for going to the rescue of 24 persons in the disabled power boat *Neptune* which was in serious danger when it's engine failed in a heavy sea.

Commended for rescuing two men and two women when their boat caught fire on July 4th. His son also assisted in the rescue.

•1913–Rescued two men and a woman.

•1914–Rescued the crew of the gas boat *Alice W.*

•1915–Assisted a grounded gasoline launch.

•1916–Assisted in getting stranded steamer off reef.

•1920–Towed disabled launch *Helena* to Menominee, Michigan.

–Towed the disabled yacht *Vanity* to Menominee, Michigan.

•1921–Rendered assistance to the disabled fishing tug *Loyd*. Made temporary repairs at the station, then towed her to Marinette, Wisconsin.[4]

Keeper Drew retired from the Service on March 31, 1929. He died suddenly of heart trouble on February 2, 1931. His death marked the end of an era on the Great Lakes, and keepers came from all parts of the Great Lakes to attend his funeral. His casket was carried by the first assistant of Menominee Light, keeper of the Menominee Light, first assistant of Green Bay Light, retired keeper of Grand Marais (Michigan) Light, keeper of the Poverty Island Light, and Edward Cornell, who replaced Frank at Green Island. He was buried with his wife at Woodlawn Cemetery in Marinette, Wisconsin. Their grave is marked with a red granite headstone engraved with a lighthouse.

Frank Drew. U.S. Coast Guard photo.

Frank and Mary Drew's headstone. Marinette Marine Corporation photo.

Footnotes

1. George R. Putnam, *Lighthouse and Lightships of the United States* (New York: Houghton-Mifflin, 1917), p. 186.

2. New clipping, n.d.

3. Clipping File.

4. *Annual Report of the Commissioner of Lighthouses, various issues* (Washington, DC: Government Printing Office): *Great Lakes Light List*, U.S. Department of Commerce, 1970, pp. 116-117; *Lighthouse Service Bulletin,* 1912, pp. 36, 40; "Naming File", U.S. Coast Guard Historian's Office; Thomas C. Pleger, *Green Island Light-Station, Wisconsin, A Synthesis of Related Historical and Archaeological Data*, 1992, unpublished manuscript, pp. 9-27.

The Frank Drew *underway past the Menominee Pierhead Light, where his father was once keeper. Marinette Marine Corporation photo.*

VIII
Anthony Petit
The Wave!

Lighthouses are usually thought of as being calm and peaceful places. Yet, they are often ravaged by storm and gale. Once in a very great while the entire structure can be completely destroyed as happened at Key West and Sand Key in the 1846 hurricane. But even then it was a slow process, a storm building in intensity until the tower is overwhelmed by the increasing force of wind and wave. The Scotch Cap disaster was very much of a "bird of a different feather."

Scotch Cap Light was located on Unimak Island, Alaska–a barren, wind swept hunk of Arctic hell. There is not a single tree on the island, and Kodiak bears and wolves are prevalent. It was the largest island on the 900-mile-long Aleutian chain that cuts southwest from Alaska toward Asia. From the beginnings of navigation, Unimak Island has been feared by sailors. Russian sailors called it "the roof of hell," from the many smoking volcanoes they saw on it. Others named it "the isle of lost ships." Vessels of every nationality fell victim to its hazards.

Behind the Cape Sarichef Station is a spot called "Graveyard Hill." In 1918, a tender arrived to take a sick keeper to hospital. In an attempt to land a boat on the beach to pick him up, it capsized, drowning the entire nine-man crew. Their bodies and that of the keeper are buried in the lonely Alaskan graveyard.

Off to the west is Unimak Pass, a wide, heavily-traversed passage between the North Pacific Ocean and Bering Sea. To keep this passage safe, two Coast Guard light stations were established. Scotch Cap Light faced the

Scotch Cap circa 1914. The buildings in the foreground were intended to have lightkeeper's families, although the station was so remote they were never allowed to come to the island. U.S. Coast Guard photo.

Construction of the new Scotch Cap Lighthouse.U.S. Coast Guard photo.

Pacific, and Cape Sarichef, 17 miles to the northward, looked out toward the Bering Sea. Both are among the most isolated stations within the Coast Guard's jurisdiction. When civilian keepers manned them, they were given a year's leave every four years served. Families were not permitted at either station.

The first Scotch Cap was built in 1903, and was the earliest manned navigational aid on the outside coast of Alaska. Its 31,000-candlepower light was visible for 15 miles and critical for sailors.

In 1940, the original 45-foot-high wooden octagonal tower was replaced by a modern 60-foot-high tower in a reinforced concrete structure built to withstand the most powerful storms. The focal plane was 93 feet above the sea and its 80,000-candlepower beacon sent a powerful beam far across the cold, wind swept sea. At the same time, Direction Finder (D/F) and diaphone foghorn facilities were also constructed. Scotch Cap recorded as much as 1,346 hours of fog a year. The foghorn was placed at the light station. The D/F station was built on the 100-foot-high bluff above the lightstation.

Duty at the lightstation was hard. Mail and supplies were delivered only every two months and if the ocean was too rough, it could be a lot longer before they finally arrived. To help fight the morale problem of such isolated duty, the station had an excellent recreation room and large galley. The men at the D/F station frequently came down to the light for a game of pool or cards.

The finished product. U.S. Coast Guard photo.

April 1, 1946, April Fools Day, back in the "Lower 48," was the day of reckoning for the crew at Scotch Cap. At the light that fateful day were five Coast Guardsmen:

–Chief Boatswain's Mate Anthony L. Petit, a 20 year veteran from Hancock, Michigan. Friends remembered he once said, "I hope to serve at as many Coast Guard ships and stations as I can before retiring in 10 years." He had enlisted in the Coast Guard in 1926 and was not married.

–Seaman First Class Dewey Dykstra of Artesia, California, was a Pacific War veteran, serving on a Coast Guard manned patrol frigate during the invasion of the Philippines.

–Fireman First Class Jack Colvin, age 20, was a native Alaskan from Juneau who enlisted in 1943. He previously served on the cutters *Atlanta* and *Clover*.

–Seaman First Class Paul J. Ness, was from Seattle, Washington.

–Motor Machinists Mate Second Class Leonard Pickering, age 25, was from Shreveport, Louisiana.

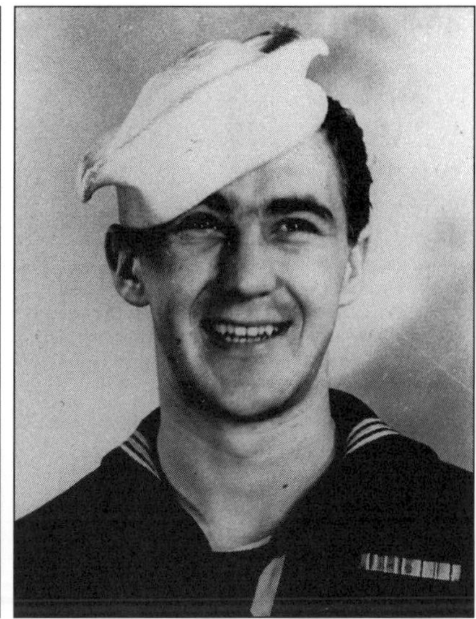

Left: Chief Boatswain's Mate Anthony Petit. Right: Fireman First Class Jack Colvin. U.S. Coast Guard photos.

Up to 0129, on April 1, all was quiet at Scotch Cap Light–just a continuation of the deadly monotony the men were so used to experiencing. The following excerpts are from a memorandum kept by Chief Radio Electrician Hoban B. Sanford, the commander of the D/F station:

> At 0130 Xray, 1 April, 1946, at which time I was awake and reading, a severe earthquake was felt. The building… creaked and groaned loudly. Objects were shaken from my locker shelves. Duration of quake was approximately 30-35 seconds. The weather was clear and calm.
>
> Knowing that the volcanoes to Northward of the building had been active at one time, I immediately looked in that direction for signs of renewed activity and upon seeing none made a routine round of the building to see what, if any, damage had been caused by the tremor. Inspection failed to reveal any damage other than objects shaken from locker shelves. The crew was all awakened by the quake.
>
> Intending to call Scotch Cap Lightstation on the phone to ascertain if they had felt, or been damaged by, the quake, I went to the phone in Operations, but Pitts, RM2, had already done so and he stated they had felt the tremor and that Pickering, MoMM2c, who was on watch at the lightstation, had said that he was "plenty scared" and was going to call Dutch Harbor Navy Radio to see what information that unit might have regarding the earthquake.

At 0157 Xray a second severe quake was felt. This one was shorter in duration, lasting approximately 15- 20 seconds, but harder than at 0130 Xray. I again looked towards the mountains for any signs of volcanic activity, but still could see none. I made a second round of the building to see if any damages had resulted but none was apparent.

The crew was gathered in the Recreation Hall discussing the shocks, their probable cause and the location when a crew member stated he had talked with Scotch Cap Lightstation after the second shock and they were attempting to contact Dutch Harbor Radio for any news of the quake.

At 0218 Xray a terrible roaring sound was heard followed almost immediately by a very heavy blow against the side of the building and

When the tidal wave passed, the lighthouse was destroyed! U.S. Coast Guard photo.

Wreckage was driven up to the top of the cliff. U.S. Coast Guard photo.

> about 3 inches of water appeared in the galley, Recreation Hall and passageway. From the time the noise was heard until the sea struck was a matter of seconds. I should say between five and ten seconds at most. Ordering the crew to get to higher ground of the DP D/F building immediately. I went to the control room and after a couple of calls to Kodiak and Adak Net Control Stations, broadcast a priority message stating we had been struck by a tidal wave and might have to abandon the station, and that I believed Scotch Cap Lightstation was lost.
>
> Received no answer to calls or receipt for message and did not know until daylight that the receiving antenna had been carried away. Electric power was fluctuating badly and starting for generator room to ascertain the cause and extent of damage, I found that D'Agostino, and Campanaro, Rm2c had voluntarily remained behind to assist.

Sanford and his men soon repaired the generators and restored full power. Throughout the night the D/F men waited for a second, bigger wave. They could plainly hear smaller waves striking the beach below the bluff. When it looked like the sea was calmer, at least temporarily, Sanford brought his men back to the D/F station for more clothing and supplies, then sent them back to the safety of higher ground. They would return to the D/F station at daylight. His memo continues:

> At 0345 I went to the edge of the hill above Scotch Cap Lightstation to observe conditions there. The way was littered with debris and the lightstation had been completely destroyed. At 0700 went down to the site of the lightstation, the sea by this time having receded to its usual limits and in company with several crew members searched among the debris for any signs of bodies or personnel. On top of hill behind the station we found a human foot, amputated at the ankle, some small bits of intestine which were apparently from a human being, and what seemed to be a human knee cap. Nothing else was found. At 0800 sent out searching parties to attempt to locate any trace of Scotch Cap personnel. Searching parties returned and reported no trace of lightstation crew.
>
> Searching parties were out daily when ever weather permitted until 20 April when CBM Sievers of CGC *Clover*, which was establishing a temporary light on the site of the destroyed light, located a body which was identified as Paul J. Ness, Clc, a member of the lightstation crew.[1] The body was viewed by several crew members and myself and all agreed that it was Ness, who had high cheek bones, slightly prominent upper incisor teeth and a small goatee. The remains were wrapped in an old blanket and canvas and removed to above the high water mark, pending burial instructions …On 22 April at 1030 CBM Sievers, who was conducting a search to the eastward, returned to unit …and stated he had found another body. With several crew members I proceeded on to the location, but was unable to identify the body. The body was decapitated, disemboweled and in a poor state of preservation.
>
> At 1100 crew members who had been searching to westward reported they had found the right thigh and foot of a man. The foot could not be identified. These remains were gathered in old mail sacks and placed in a rough coffin. The body of Ness was placed in an individual coffin.
>
> At 1545 23 April, the body of Ness was buried in an individual grave, the unidentified portions of bodies buried in a common grave adjacent thereto. The graves are at the seaward edge of the western bank of the first ravine to the eastward of Scotch Cap Lightstation and are approximately 300 yards from the site of the light, near the graves of

The lighthouse was nearly completely smashed. U.S. Coast Guard photos.

> the Russian seamen.[2] The graves are plainly marked with white wooden crosses with brass plates securely attached, and are well covered with rocks to discourage depredation by animals.
>
> The area covered by searches was approximately 5 miles eastward, 4 miles westward from Scotch Cap Lightstation and inland to the high water mark of the tidal wave.[3]

Scientists determined the second tremor apparently caused a massive segment of the Aleutian Trench wall to collapse, sending a shock waves speeding to the surface and a deadly series of tsunamis or tidal waves went speeding out in all directions! Unfortunately for Unimak Island and the men at Scotch Cap Lightstation, it was directly in the way of the tidal wave and would be first hit. Tidal waves are very low waves that travel very fast, at speeds up to 500 miles per hour in the deep water. When they move into shallow water, the speed decreases quickly, but the height increases to

The Coast Guard quickly established a temporary automated light. U.S. Coast Guard photo.

In July 1971, the new Scotch Cap Light was fully automated and men no longer had to endure the desolation of Scotch Cap. U.S. Coast Guard photo.

upwards of 100 feet. Scientists later determined that the epicenter was about 70 miles southeast of Unimak, deep in the dark depths of the Aleutian Trench.

For 11 consecutive days following the disaster, the D/F log recorded tremors and quakes of varying degrees. Although tremors are commonplace in the Aleutians, they were always unnerving. Although no one from the D/F station saw the tidal wave strike the lightstation, the scene can easily be imagined. As the wave approached the island, its speed dropped quickly, but height increased dramatically. As it reached the beach, it towered more than a 100 feet into the air. With a tremendous roar, hundreds of thousands of tons of water crashed on to the beach and slammed into the station. The building collapsed as if it were smashed with a giant hammer. Men and property were shattered into hopeless pieces, torn apart by the insane intensity of the great wave. The men were certainly killed instantly by the gruesome grinding of concrete and metal. Piling into the bluff, it climbed the sheer rock and part of the wave swept over the top, reaching the D/F station and flooding it, then sliding back into the sea.

Two sections of the Anthony Petit *being joined during construction. Marinette Marine Corporation photo.*

The sea quake that caused the Scotch Cap tsunami, sent other waves crashing ashore throughout the Pacific. In Hawaii alone approximately 160 lives were lost because of them.

In 1950, a new Scotch Cap Lightstation was built. The modern light was 116 feet above sea level and the crews quarters on much higher and safer ground. The light was automated in July, 1971. No longer would men be exposed to the numbing isolation of Unimak Island.

There are two also ghost stories attached to Scotch Cap Light. After the Scotch Cap disaster and the light was rebuilt, it suffered a failure of both electrical generators. Without power the beam was out, and an official "Notice to Mariners" was broadcast to all shipping informing them of the darkened beacon. A Coast Guard cutter cruising offshore while this happened plainly saw the light on! When it radioed to the light to ask why the "notice" was broadcast if the light was working, the sailors at the station were dumfounded. The light was still off! What had the men on the cutter seen? No official explanation was ever offered.

Fitting her Alaskan namesake, the Anthony Petit *splashes into an ice covered river. Marinette Marine Corporation photo.*

Scotch Cap is also haunted by "Jake," a ghost that reportedly enjoys playing pranks. Jake has never caused harm. But the lights that flick on and off, doors opening and closing and strange noises in the night, all were Jake's hallmarks.

A keeper was once removed from nearby Cape Sarichef Light because he went "over the edge" and started muttering incessantly about being visited by the ghost of dead Aleuts murdered by Russian fur hunters.

Today the remains of the old station can still be located at the base of the bluff. It stands as a silent and eerie memorial to the lightkeepers who died while doing their lonely job.

BMC Petit was typical of the men and women who served at remote and lonely stations. They did it for love of country and the certain knowledge that others depended on them, not for fame or glory. Sometimes they had to make the supreme sacrifice. Although not in the fury of war, BMC Petit and his men added their names to the Coast Guard's gallant history.[4]

Footnotes

1. Coast Guard Cutter *Clover*, was a 180-foot buoy tender stationed in Dutch Harbor, Alaska and used for aids to navigation support.

2. The sailors are from World War II wreck of the Russian freighter *Turksib*, which went aground near the station. The captain and one crewman were killed in the disaster. Severe storms kept rescuers from removing the 60 survivors from the light for several weeks.

3. "Memorandum, Chief Radio Electrician Hoban B. Sanford, USCG."

4. Hans Christian Adamson, *Keepers of the Lights* (New York: Greenberg, 1955), pp. 249-256; "Clipping File,: RG-26, NARA; James A. Gibbs, Jr., *Sentinels of the North Pacific* (Portland, Oregon: Binfords and Mort, 1955), pp. 201-221; "Log of Station 368;" "Naming File," U.S. Coast Guard Historian's Office; "Scotch Cap Lighthouse," [http://www.usalights.com/alaska/scotchcap.htm], February 14, 1999; "Scotch Cap Lighthouse Disaster," [http://www.teleport.com/~alany/uscg/ltsa.html], February 14, 1999; Michael J. Mooney, "Tidal Wave," *Alaska* (June 1976); Don Rutherford, "Disaster at Scotch Cap," *Keepers Log,* Winter 1986, pp. 12-14; Robert L. Scheina, *U.S. Coast Guard Cutters and Craft, 1946-90* (Annapolis, MD: U.S. Naval Institute Press, 1990) pp. 150-152.

IX
Barbara Mabrity Of Key West

As explained in the chapter on Joshua Appleby, Key West was an important port, not only for general merchant shipping and the wrecking fleet, but also as a base for the U.S. Navy. When Lieutenant Commander Matthew Perry sailed into the harbor in the schooner *Shark* in March 1822, he immediately recognized both the importance of the harbor, as well as the critical need for a lighthouse. At the end of the month he sent a report to the Secretary of the Navy recommending four lighthouses be built along the Florida coast. Congress authorized only two, at Cape Florida and the Dry Tortugas, but it wasn't until May 26, 1824 that funds were appropriated for construction.

When Commodore Porter arrived the following year to build a permanent naval base, he wrote it was "…the best harbor within the limits of the United States or its territories, to the south of the Chesapeake."

In April 1824, Lieutenant James Ramage of the U.S. Navy sent another report to the Secretary of the Navy, strongly endorsing a lighthouse at Key West. When Congress finally appropriated the funds for the original two lighthouses in May of that year, it added funding for a third, "…on one of the Sambo Keys." The Sambos are three islets about seven miles from Key West harbor, on the Atlantic side of the island. In July a contract was let with a Samuel Lincoln of Hingham, Massachusetts, for construction of the three lighthouses. As normal, Winslow Lewis was to provide the lighting apparatus, 15 lamps with 15- or 16-inch parabolic reflectors.

While in route to Florida in September to inspect the sites prior to construction, Lincoln's ship was overwhelmed by a hurricane and lost with all hands. It took a while for Lincoln's firm to recover from the disaster, but by mid-December a schooner arrived in Key West with the contractor's representatives. After meeting with the government agent, a site for the Cape Florida Light was selected. When the government man went to Key West to determine the site for the Sambo Keys light, he discovered the construction crew already at work, not on one of the Sambo Keys, but at Key West. It seems the contractor's representative had waited a month for the government agent to arrive and grew impatient with the delay. Commodore Porter took advantage of the opportunity to press for construction of the light at Key West's Whitehead Point instead of the distant Sambo Keys. Porter knew that at high tide the Sambos were completely covered and he thought them a poor location for a lighthouse. Knowing that "time is money" and after all, Commodore Porter did represent the government, too, the contractor set to work.

Commodore Porter later wrote to the agent:

> I am clearly and decidedly of opinion that if the light house is to be made of any other than wooden materials there is not suitable situation for in the neighborhood, but the point of this island, called Whiteheads Point and I am also of opinion, that if the light can be seen clearly and distinctly at the distance of fifteen miles, the object of warning vessels that approach the reef, will be as well effected, as though the light house was on one of the small keys called Sambos or on Sand Key–with this advantage, that it will prove a sure and certain guide to vessels bound to this place and crossing the reef at night, the bearing of Whiteheads point, being taken as the best for crossing the bar.[1]

By the time the government agent arrived, crews had the walls and rafters of the dwelling up and several feet of the lighthouse foundation. Commodore Porter had his "fait accompli." The lighthouse would be built at Key West. After a delay caused by illness among the workers, the lighthouse was finished just after January 1, 1826. The lighthouse was an impressive building for primitive Key West. The whitewashed brick tower from base to lantern was 47 feet tall. Considering the height of the ground, the light was 83 feet above the sea. For a generation it was the tallest structure at Key West.

Michael Mabrity, a harbor pilot from St. Augustine, was appointed the first keeper at a yearly salary of $400.[2] As common for the times, he received his official appointment signed by President John Quincy Adams. His wife, Barbara, was appointed as assistant keeper.

The Key West Lighthouse first exhibited a light on January 13, 1826. Because of the poor quality of the oil provided by Winslow Lewis, problems were encountered requiring frequent trimming and excessive smoking. Mabrity had to work extra hard to keep the light useable. Within months, several of the cheaply-made parabolic reflectors had lost their silver plating, further degrading the light. By the following spring the smoking problems were overcome with a new, high-quality oil and the bad reflectors replaced.

Apparently Mabrity grew bored of just being a lightkeeper. He became active in town government, and in 1828 was elected to the city council. Because Whitehead Point was too far from the center of town, he purchased a home in the city and moved his family there. He arranged for a hired man to take care of the light in his absence. The problem eventually was "bucked-up" to Pleasonton, who ordered Mabrity to move back to the lighthouse and assume his full duties. Mabrity complied and later had his salary increased to $500 yearly.

As a lighthouse keeper Mabrity was an important member of Key West society, he often was visited by noted travelers. For example, in 1832 he and Barbara entertained the famous naturalist John James Audubon who was in the area on a field trip.

Yellow fever was the scourge of the tropics and cost many early Key Westers their lives. In May 1832, the dreaded disease took Michael Mabrity. Barbara was appointed keeper in his stead. The decision was less a reflection of her competence as it was of providing an income for her and her six fatherless children.

Now Barbara was the only person to perform all of the lighthouse duties–to polish and clean the lamps and reflectors, keep the grounds and tend the light through the long dark nights. There was no assistant.

Death was a constant companion to the early settlers of Key West. Not only did the deadly peril of yellow fever walk the dusty streets, but Indian attack was not uncommon. In 1835 a small contingent of soldiers under the command of Major Francis Dade were present in Key West to protect it against raids by the Seminoles. Doubtless in such a small community, Barbara knew many of the men and their families. When attacks increased to the north, the small troop was ordered north and was massacred by the Indians between Tampa and Ocala. Barbara, as well as many others in Key West, must have grieved for the brave men.

Indian attacks at New Smyra, north of Cape Canaveral, Mosquito Inlet (Ponce de Leon Inlet), New River (Fort Lauderdale), Cape Florida and Indian Key, drove surviving settlers south to Key West. To help protect the city, the Navy deployed the famous frigate *Constitution* to the city as well as another vessel. The city also extended the lighthouse road a quarter mile east to assist in spotting Indians approaching from that direction. Living far out of the main part of town, such measures must have helped ease Barbara's mind, especially considering her children. The Seminole War lasted until 1842.

Throughout the hostilities, Barbara continued to maintain the light. A group of local citizens wrote Pleasonton to call his attention to "…the circumstances that Mrs. Mabrity, the keeper of the light upon this island, has for a number of years performed the duties of her office with fidelity and to the satisfaction …of the Collector and Navigators; that she has practiced and still practices rigid economy in her mode of living and yet she has not been able to accumulate any property to support her in her old age; that she is less able to perform the labor and endure the fatigue of her office that she has been, and that in our opinion a just appreciation of her past services, and her present situation give her an equitable claim up the government for assistance."[3] Nevertheless, no help was given to Barbara. It wasn't until 1854, when she was 72 years old, that she received an assistant keeper. The Collector of Customs for the Key West district reported, that the Key West lighthouse was "…as usual, efficient and well kept."

When Barbara lit the lamps at sunset on October 10, 1846, she must have known that a major storm was brewing. She had kept the lamps burning through severe hurricanes in 1831, 1835, 1841 and 1842. Surely she would make it through another one.

By the next morning, when she was high up in the lamp room preparing them for the next night's use, heavy rain was already driving hard into the tower, propelled by a screaming wind. There was no doubt it was a full-fledged hurricane–and a bad one to boot!

Believing the brick tower was stronger than their own homes, a number of townspeople fled to the lighthouse for shelter. Barbara welcomed them all to the safety of the tower. Her children also come back to the light to help their mother during the storm.

Lieutenant Pease on the *Morris*, later wrote that after the hurricane finally passed, there was complete devastation in its wake. His ship was surrounded by "…wrecks of all descriptions: one ship on her beam ends, three brigs dismasted, also three schooners: three vessels sunk… four vessels bottom up. How many persons attached to these vessels I am unable to say. We have picked up only two… The light-house at Key West and Sand Key washed away, and Key West is in ruins. A white sand beach covers the spot where Key West lighthouse stood… The only vestige of the light-house to be seen is a portion of the iron posts of the lantern and some pieces of soap stone which have washed one hundred yards from the spot where they fell.[4]"

The new lighthouse at Key West was built further inland. U.S. Coast Guard photo.

When townspeople went out to where the lighthouse was they found it totally destroyed. Barbara was the sole survivor. All of the townspeople and five of her children were dead, killed by the fury of the hurricane. Fourteen bodies were eventually recovered, including her offspring. Only one had survived the disaster. Stephen Mallory, the Key West Collector of Customs, claimed it was the most destructive hurricane "…of any that has ever visited these islands."

A temporary light was established on Whiteheads Point in place of the destroyed lighthouse. Consisting of a tripod with a large signal lantern raised 30 feet high. It too, was to be kept by Barbara.

The new lighthouse was built on a small hill further inland. Barbara was appointed as keeper. To provide shelter during the construction of the new tower, a small dismantled wooden story-and-a-half house was brought down to Key West on the vessel *Honey*. As related in the chapter on Joshua Appleby, the *Honey* was used as a lightship until the Sand Key Lighthouse could be rebuilt.

The keeper's house, built in 1829, had a parlor, dining room, two bedrooms and an attic. A detached kitchen was out back to both help with keeping the house cooler in the tropic heat and act as a safeguard against fire. A privy was built to the west while a 13-foot-deep, 4000-gallon brick cistern was cut deep into the limestone north of the house to provide a safe storage for fresh water.

Lightkeeping duties for Mabrity became a little easier when William Richardson was named her assistant. He served from 1854-60, his place being taken by an Edwin Halseman. As Barbara aged, having assistants was very important.

Barbara held the position as keeper until 1864. When she left at age 82, she had been the Key West keeper for 38 years. There is an old story that she was well-known as a quiet Southern sympathizer during the Civil War. Indeed, virtually the entire population of Key West were rebels and the state did vote for secession. Doubtless the presence of Fort Zachary Taylor and the Navy base kept the city under Union control. It was the only Florida port never to come under the control of the Confederates. After she made a remark considered disloyal to the Union that was overheard by an assistant and reported to the military, she was asked to retire. She refused to do so, and in official records is listed as "removed."

When Barbara died in 1867, she was quietly buried in the Key West cemetery.

Key West Light remained lit throughout the Civil War. Had Barbara been a really strong Confederate, she could have smashed the lens and darkened the tower. Early in the war Confederates had removed the lenses from Jupiter Light, St. Augustine, and Cape Canaveral. Others attacked the light at Cape Florida, smashing the lens. To protect the Key West Light, the Navy often stationed guards around it.

Barbara, as a member of one of the oldest families in St. Augustine, was probably a Confederate at heart. But she took the Oath of Allegiance to the Union and kept her job until her disloyal remark.

The new lighthouse was built in 1849. Originally 47 feet tall, the tower was later raised 20 feet to increase visibility against a growing city skyline. It was still equipped with Lewis equipment, 13 lamps with 21-inch parabolic reflectors. In 1858, a third order Fresnel lens replaced the outmoded Lewis contraption. Cleaning and maintaining the Fresnel was much easier than the complicated Lewis equipment. It was a good thing the Fresnel required less maintenance, because six years earlier the Lighthouse Board had installed a series of buoys to help ships navigate to and from the harbor. Maintaining them was a job given to the Key West lightkeeper.

The walls at the base of the new brick tower were four and a half feet thick and tapered to two and a half at the top. Like the old tower, the new one was also whitewashed. Hurricanes continued to slam into Key West. In 1866 the light received considerable damage from one.

Sometime prior to 1918, the light was converted to acetylene gas and automated. In 1934 it was electrified, and in 1970 discontinued as active aid to navigation. Today, the property is owned by the Key West Arts and Historical Society.

Mabrity also established a lighthouse dynasty. A granddaughter married John Carroll, who became keeper in 1870, and she became keeper on his death in 1889. She didn't hold the position long because later in the year another grandson, William Bethel, became keeper. When he was made an invalid after a fall from the tower in 1908, his wife became keeper and his son the assistant. She served until the light was automated in 1915. The Mabritys, their grandchildren, and their grandchildren's spouses served as keepers of the Key West Light for 82 of the 89 years in was manned![5]

The Barbara Mabrity *will carry on the heroic tradition of her namesake. Marinette Marine Corporation photo.*

Footnotes

1. "Lighthouse Superintendents Letter File," RG 26, NARA.

2. It is interesting to speculate on his appointment. In an 1823 petition for the appointment of a federal marshall, he appears as a Miquel Mabrity. Given the high Spanish population of St. Augustine, was he an Anglo Michael that became a Latino Miguel in St. Augustine, or a Latino Miquel that became an Anglo, Michael in Key West?

3. "Lighthouse File,'" RG 26, NARA.

4.*New York Daily Tribune,* November 2, 1846.

5. *Annual Reports,* U.S. Lighthouse Service, 1838-1909 "Key West Lighthouse," [http://bansemer.cftnet.com/FL-lighthouse/Key%20West.htm] February 12, 1999; "Lighthouse File," RG 26, NARA; "Lighthouse Superintendents File," RG 26, NARA; *New York Daily Tribune,* November 2, 1846; John K. Mahon. *History of the Second Seminole War,* 1834-1842. (Gainsville, FL: The University of Florida Press, 1967), pp. 82-101; "Naming File," U.S. Coast Guard Historian's Office, Washington DC: Thomas W. Taylor, The First Key West Lighthouse," *The Keepers Log,* Vol. XI, No. 3 (Spring 1995), pp. 16-22; Thomas W. Taylor, The Second Key West Lighthouse," *The Keeper's Log,* Vol. XI, No. 4 (Summer 1995), pp. 2-15.

X

Maria Bray
The Twin Towers of Cape Ann

Many lighthouse keepers have been honored for keeping their lights burning through the midst of a roaring storm. But think of poor Maria Bray, wife of the keeper of the Cape Ann Lights, and the terrible ordeal she went through.

The lights were actually on Thacher Island, just off the Massachusetts coast. The island was named for Captain Anthony Thacher, an Englishmen whose vessel, the *Watch and Wait*, wrecked in a ferocious storm near the

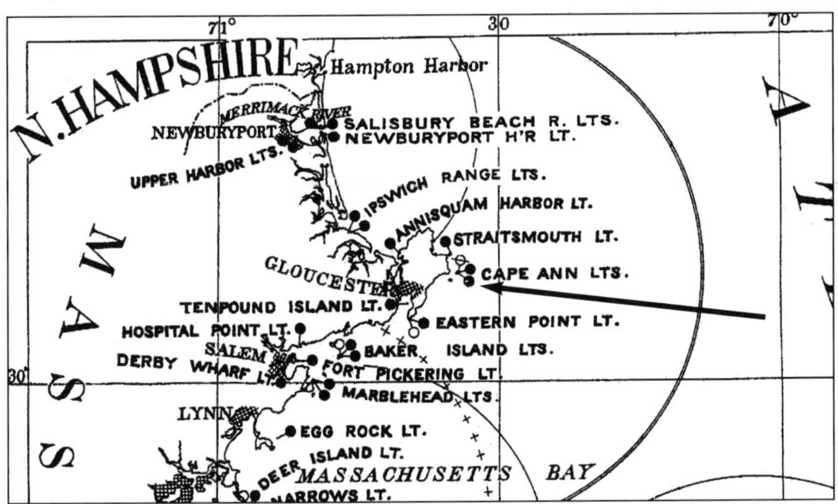

island in 1635. He originally named the island "Thacher's Woe." Thacher and his wife, Elizabeth, were the only survivors of the wreck in which 21 people perished. Thus inspiring the name. Thacher was given the island to recompense him for his losses and it remained in his family for 80 years.

On April 22, 1771, the Province of Massachusetts Bay Council authorized the erection of twin towers on the island. It was the first light built to mark a danger spot that wasn't located at a harbor entrance.

The original act providing for the building of the lighthouse clearly established the need:

> Whereas the headland of Cape Ann projects itself into the main ocean in such a manner as to form two deep bays - one, to the northward, commonly called Ipswich Bay; and another, to the southward, called the Massachusetts Bay - that there are two very dangerous ledges of rocks which lay off from the headland which, for want of some guide, frequently prove fatal to vessels, and it being generally thought that a lighthouse, or house erected on Thachers Island, or the mainland of Cape Ann, would be very serviceable to the navigation and commerce of this province and be a means of preserving the lives and estates of a great number of His Majesty's subjects by directing the distressed in stormy and tempestuous weather into safe harbor.[1]

The original keeper, a Captain Kirkwood, was a Tory and removed by the Patriots during the Revolutionary War with the result that the lights were dark until 1793. The lightstation was among those turned over to the Federal Government in 1789. Thacher Island was considered a very important station. In 1810, the south tower became the second lighthouse, after Boston Light, to receive an Argand lamp and parabolic reflector. A new stone keeper's house was built in 1816, and it still stands today with modifications and additions. One of the keepers, Charles Wheeler, was especially active. He invented a type of lighthouse lamp that prevented oil from congealing in cold weather, planted apple and pear trees and grapevines, and cleared land. He was also active in helping shipwreck victims. The light continued to be improved. When an agent of the Portland Steam Navigation Company complained in 1853 about the lack of a fog bell, one was quickly installed.

The new Lighthouse Board took a good look at all of the nation's lights and evaluated those at Cape Ann as "...very important" and saw the need to increase their power and range. "The towers were only 45 feet high, built of very inferior materials, badly constructed and require attention, especially during the season of winter storms to keep them in fit condition for the exhibit

The twin lights at Cape Ann were considered an important part of the national lighthouse system. U.S. Coast Guard photo.

of light." At the time, each light tower had 11 lamps with 21-inch reflectors provided by Winslow Lewis.

In 1859, Congress authorized the rebuilding of the two light towers of cut granite. The work was accomplished in 1860-61. Each new tower was 124 feet tall and had a first order Fresnel lens. Considering the island's height, the lights were 164 feet above sea level.

In 1864, Alexander Bray, a disabled Civil War veteran, was given the job in partial return for his battle service. His salary was set at $1,000, a fairly large amount and likely in consideration for his service. Bray and his family were on the island for a year when Maria had her great challenge.

The day before Christmas, one of Bray's assistant keepers was struck down with a severe fever. All of Maria's home remedies were useless and could not bring the fever down. Since Bray also needed to make a supply run to the mainland, he and his other assistant loaded the sick man into the station boat and started rowing for town. Maria and her young nephew, Sidney Haskell, and her two young children, remained on the island. While the weather was not good, it was a short trip and trouble was not anticipated.

As he left the dock, Alexander told his wife he would be back just as soon as he could, probably no more than a couple of hours. But the weather in December can change fast, certainly faster than a lightkeeper can row. Maria watched carefully as the boat disappeared around the point. Within several hours a heavy snowstorm struck the island, blotting out all sight of the mainland shore. The dense snow soon reduced visibility to near zero.

Maria knew her husband and his assistant would have landed the sick keeper and headed back to the island as quickly as they could, but in the snowstorm how would they find the island? When they didn't arrive and the morning became early afternoon, she reluctantly concluded that they were likely lost at sea. The only way she could help was to fire up the lights!

The Brays had two children, a toddler named Tom and a baby still confined to a crib. Dressing Tom as warm as she could against the storm, she picked him up and headed for the north light 300 yards away. She pushed open the front door and started for the light tower. Forcing her way through snow drifts while carrying Tom was exhausting work. When she reached the tower door, she was nearly exhausted and had to pause to regain her strength. She climbed the 156 steps to the top of the 124-foot tower, stopping at each landing. In the lamp room Maria carefully trimmed the wicks and prepared to light the lamps. It was only 2:00 p.m. but she knew that since she had to run both lighthouses, as well as safeguard her children, she would be unable to keep them going unless she staggered the lighting. Carefully she struck a match and gave flame to the wick. After she wound the clockwork-like device

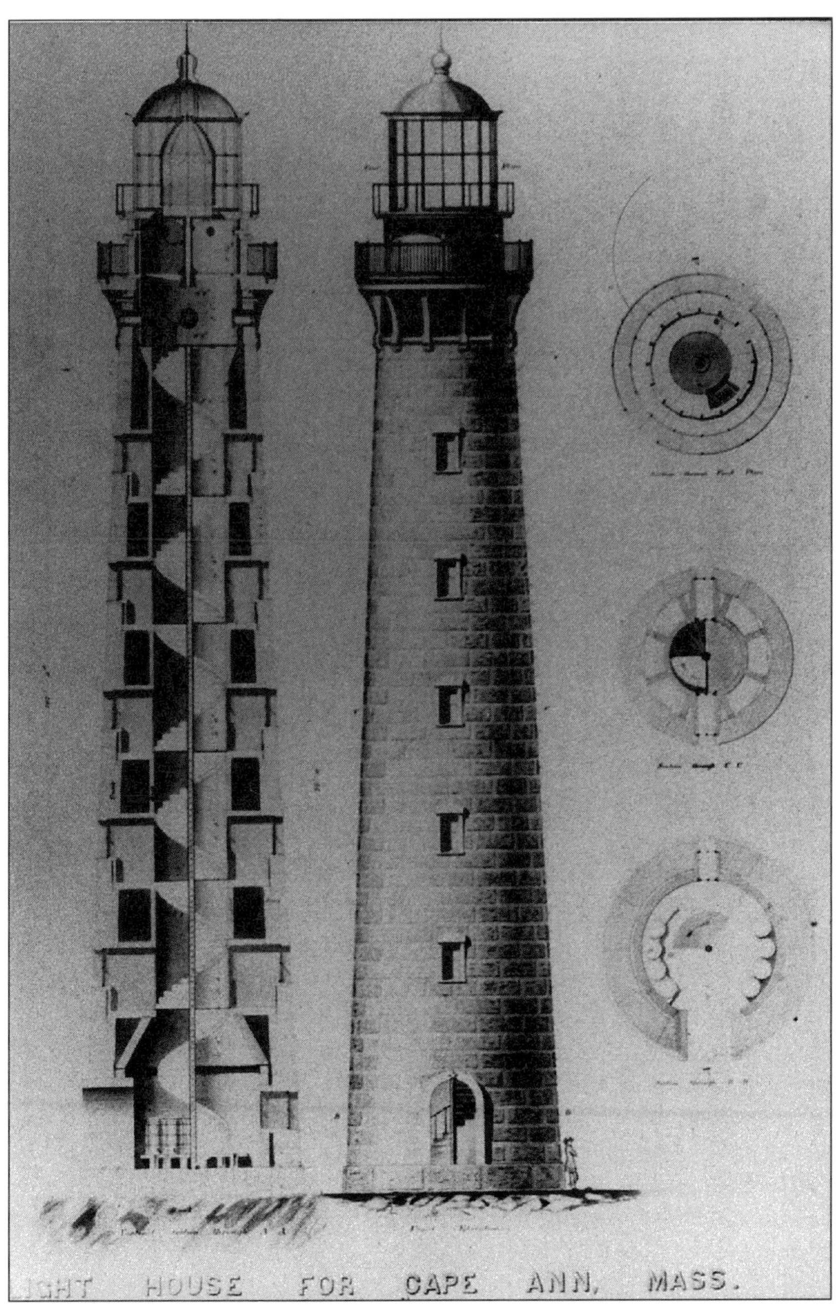

Interior arrangement of the Cape Ann Towers. U.S. Coast Guard photo.

that would provide a steady five-hour supply of oil to the lamp, she took Tom and painstakingly climbed down the spiral iron stairs to the ground.

Before sunset, she and Tom climbed the second tower, prepared and lit its light. At 7:00 p.m. it was necessary for her to return to the north tower and wind the oil-feeding clock mechanism. Since both children were sleeping peacefully, she bundled up herself in her warmest coat and boats and headed up the narrow trail. The accumulated snow was deep and hard to struggle through. She had to fight her way to the light, and when she arrived discovered the door was nearly buried by the snow. Finding the handle, she pushed it open and stepped inside. Again gathering her strength, she slowly climbed the steps to the lamp room. After checking the wicks, she wound the clockwork and returned down the stairs. Again she rested before battling back to the house. All night long she repeated the ritual, fighting her way through the blizzard to the north tower, checking the wicks, winding the mechanism and struggling back to the house and second tower where the process was repeated.

By 5:00 a.m. her strength was gone and sitting down in a comfortable chair, Maria fell asleep, fatigued from her superhuman efforts. A short time later the snow finally stopped and her husband spotted the bright beams of the twin lights. At 7:00 a.m. he reached the island and was soon safe at home. In the absence of all three keepers, Maria had kept the lights burning. It was reported that when he woke Maria, she asked him if the lights were still burning. His reply was, "If they were not, I would not be here!"

Even with the twin towers, many shipwrecks still happened in the vicinity of the island. In 1876, a steamer carrying coal struck a submerged wreck in a storm. The local residents salvaged more than 500 tons of coal and severely limited their winter fuel bills. A tragedy occurred on October 20, 1891, when Assistant Keeper John Farley was killed trying to land at the boat slip in heavy seas. In November 1898, a terrific storm struck the New England coast. Many ships were wrecked in the tempestuous seas. The most famous of these was the sidewheel steamer *Portland*, lost with around 200 people aboard. Albert Whitten, the assistant keeper at Thacher Island, may have been the last person to see the big steamer as in was foundering in storm-tossed Massachusetts Bay.

The light station had another brush with fame. In 1919, when President Wilson was returning to the United States on the S. S. *America*, the vessel narrowly escaped the rocks near the island in a fog. Only the timely blasts of the horn, heard at the last minute, allowed the captain to change his course in time to avoid striking them.

The Maria Bray *during construction. It is a great example of Marinette Marine quality. Marinette Marine Corporation photo.*

The North Light was eliminated in 1932 as an economy measure. In 1980, the Coast Guard removed the last crews and automated the remaining South Light and fog whistle. The Thacher Island Association, a concerned group of Cape Ann citizens, was formed in 1983 to help save the lights. In 1989, the North Light was restored and opened to the public. It has since been relighted as a private aid to navigation, thus making Thacher Island the only operating twin light station in the United States.[2]

Footnotes

1. *Coast Guard Bulletin*, November 1939, p. 32.

2. "A Bit of History," [http://www1.shore.net/%7Egfisher/tia/history,htm], February 14, 1999; *Annual Report*, U.S. Lighthouse Service, various years; "Clipping File", RG 26, NARA; "Naming File," Coast Guard Historian's Office.

XI

Henry Blake
Indian Trouble At New Dungeness

Lighthouse keepers are traditionally thought of as having to fight storm, fog and other seaborne enemies. But Henry Blake of New Dungeness Lighthouse had to withstand an Indian assault!

When illuminated in 1857, New Dungeness was the first lighthouse in the Strait of Juan de Fuca and the first north of Cape Disappointment at the mouth of the Columbia River. The lighthouse sits at the bitter end of a desolate, five-and-a-half-mile-long sand spit that is considered the longest natural sand spit in the United States. An old description of it said the light consisted of:

> …a keeper's dwelling of stone of a grayish yellow color, with a tower of brick 89 feet high and rising 65 feet therefrom. It is the frustum of a cone, of which the upper half is painted black and the lower half white. But when seen from the northward at some miles, the dark-gray dwelling makes the tower appear to have a lower dark band. The tower is surmounted by and iron lantern, painted red; the height of the focal plane is one hundred feet above the sea. The light, burning lard oil, was first exhibited December 1, 1857 and shows every night from sunset to sunrise, a fixed white light of the third order of Fresnel, illuminating the entire horizon.

As if to make up for the isolation, the scenery around the light is magnificent. The shipping lanes run directly past the lighthouse and on a

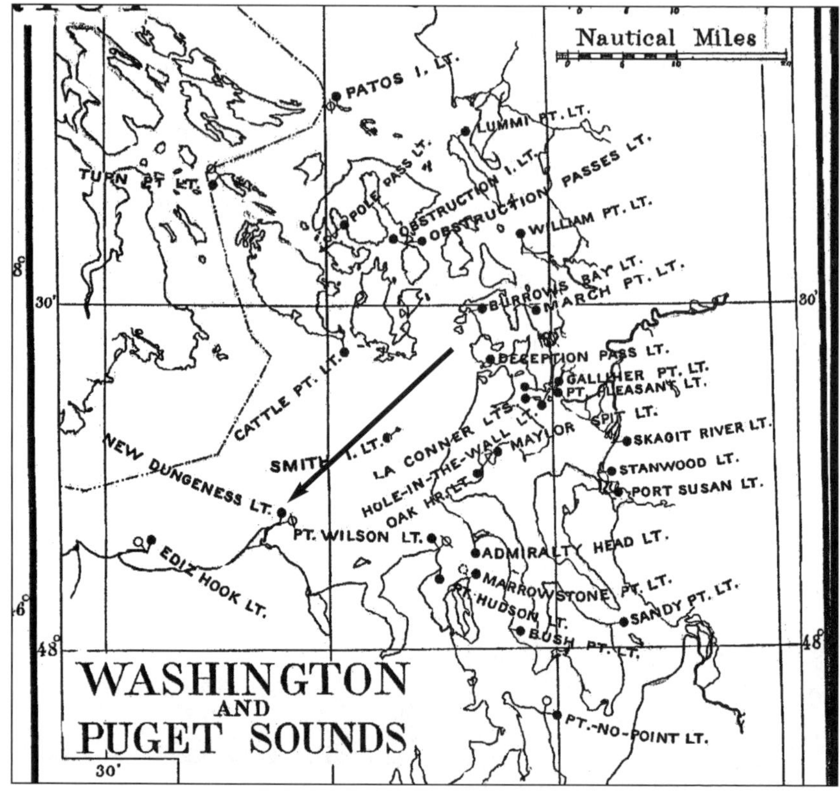

clear day the Olympic Mountains are visible to the south, the Cascade Mountains to the east, San Juan Islands to the north, and Vancouver Island to the northwest. Wildlife, including bald eagles, sea lions, hawks and seals, are plentiful.

The first keeper was Henry William Blake, a dapper-looking young bachelor with a thin moustache and goatee. His reaction on arriving at his forlorn station isn't recorded, but for a man used to the gaiety and bright lights of San Francisco, it must have been a shock indeed! After time however, he met Mary Ann McDonnell, the daughter of Richard McDonnell, a local settler. Their house was at the mainland end of the spit, but for a lonely love-struck lightkeeper, the long walk was an easy stroll. In mid-1862, Henry and Mary Ann were married and life at the lighthouse wasn't forlorn any more! Mary Ann proved a real help. Not only was she Henry's wife and mother of their five children, three of which were born at the light, but also helped with the keeper's duties when necessary.

The incident Henry is best remembered for happened in 1868. Eighteen Tsimshian Indians, including men, women and children, were peacefully camping near the lighthouse. The small band was on its way to Fort Simpson in British Columbia after picking hops in the nearby Puyallup Valley. With them was $500 in gold coins, earned picking the hops. However, they had been spotted by a group of 26 Clallam Indians, their mortal enemy. The Clallam and Tsimshian were long foes and battles between them were commonplace. Under cover of a foggy darkness, the Clallam Indians attacked! The whoops of the attackers were mixed with the screams of the confused Tsimshian into a calliope of bloody terror! Using clubs and long, sharp salmon spears, they killed all of them except one pregnant woman who feigned death. The Clallam striped the dead of all valuables, including bracelets and rings and the treasured gold coins. When the killers left, the lone survivor crawled painfully to the lighthouse and was taken in by Henry.

The New Dungeness Peninsula. The lighthouse is visible at the end. U.S. Coast Guard photo.

New Dungeness Lighthouse. U.S. Coast Guard photo.

The woman had 20 stab wounds and with the resulting loss of blood, was near death. Henry and Mary Ann put her to bed and carefully tended to her wounds.

Several hours later, the Clallam Indians realized she had escaped when they counted the dead. Following her blood trail, they went to the lighthouse and demanded Henry give her to them. Henry refused to turn her over and bravely stood his ground against the bloodthirsty band of killers. It was clear to Henry that not only were the lives of the woman and her unborn child at stake in the deadly game he was forced into playing, but also those of his own wife and children and himself. Had the Indians attacked, it is doubtful one man could have beaten them off.

Finally the Indians left, perhaps afraid of the inevitable reprisals the Army would take should they harm the lightkeeper or his family. Trouble with the Indians was nothing new. During the construction of the nearby Umpqua Lighthouse, also built in 1857, a minor battle took place between the Indians and the contractor's crew.

After the local people learned of the massacre, they buried the victims on a small spit forever known as "Graveyard Spit." Lawmen and volunteers eventually captured the attackers and all were given hard labor as their punishment.

In time the pregnant woman recovered and continued her interrupted journey to Fort Simpson on a Hudson Bay steamer. Many years later an Indian brave, the unborn son of the woman, returned to New Dungeness Light and told the keeper who he was. Henry was long gone, but the present keeper related that his son, Richard, was living in town. One story says the Indian went to find the son, but never located him. Others say the Indian left the light and just paddled off in his canoe to the Canadian side of the Straits.

In spite of his bravery, Henry was once accused of not keeping a proper fog signal. Less than a month after the Indian trouble, the bark *Atlanta* was bound out for San Francisco but went aground in thick fog and smoke. The *Atlanta* was so near the lighthouse that her captain later said he could hear the lightkeeper talking but could not hear the fog bell! The captain said he yelled to the keeper, but received no answer. When the weather cleared enough for the keeper to see the bark, he then started to ring the bell, or so claimed the captain. The *Atlanta* managed to work herself off and the captain later wrote a letter to the district superintendent complaining about the incident. Knowing that fog can indeed distort sound, making distant sound appear close and close sound appear distant, the inspector replied that while he couldn't explain the apparent lapse, he had, "...always found Mr. Blake a faithful and reliable keeper."

The Henry Blake *slowly comes together on the shop floor. Marinette Marine Corporation photo.*

Henry departed New Dungeness Light in 1869 and apparently just faded into Northwest history.

The tower at New Dungeness was one of the very few ever reduced in size. Originally 100 feet high, in 1927 it was cut down to 63 feet as the result of cracking suffered apparently from the vibrations of heavy cannon firing from a fort on the Canadian side of the strait.[1]

Footnotes

1. "Naming File," Coast Guard Historian's Office; "Lighthouse File", RG 26, NARA; "New Dungeness Lighthouse, " [http://www.maine.com/lights/dungeness.htm], February 10, 1999.

XII

George D. Cobb

Where The Fog Rolls Thick!

One of the foggiest areas in the entire Pacific Coast is at Point Bonita, California, two and a half miles west of the Golden Gate Bridge, at the outer reaches of the north entrance to San Francisco Bay. The point itself is a magnificent formation of rock that runs for a half-mile into the cold sea from the scenic Marin Highlands.

The area was plainly dangerous to mariners and many urged the construction of a lighthouse. The local superintendent of lights agreed and wrote, "The erection of a lighthouse at Bonitia Point …is of great moment and importance to the commerce of this port …and is essential to the safety of vessels approaching this harbor." Congress agreed, and in 1853 appropriated funds for construction of the light. Construction was especially difficult. Point Bonita was very remote, and landing the necessary supplies and equipment near to the Point demanding and complicated. One contractor quit outright after seeing the difficulty. A second firm persevered, and slowly the lighthouse took shape. On May 2, 1855, the second order Fresnel was illuminated for the first time.

Fog at Point Bonita averages over 1,000 hours a year, a near record amount even for the old Lighthouse Service. To warn vessels off, the Service decided it needed to use the loudest device it could find. No mere bell, regardless of size would work for Point Bonita. To fight the fog battle, they rolled out the heavy artillery–literally!

The Service obtained from the Army a surplus 24-pound cannon. Often called a "Long Tom" because of its eight-foot length, it was the same type of gun that roared defiance from the USS *Constitution* during her many magnificent sea fights with the British. To operate the gun they also hired one Sergeant Edward Maloney, a retired artillery soldier, as keeper. He was given specific instructions. "You are charged with the firing of the 24-pounder gun placed at Point Bonita as a fog signal, and will proceed thither tomorrow with the powder purchased for the same. In the performance of your duties you will be governed by the following directions: To fire the gun every half hour during fogs at the entrance to the Bay whether they occur at night or day, the firing being made at the hours and half hours of San Francisco Mean Time."

When the cannon went into service on August 8, 1856, it was the first fog signal on the Pacific Coast. It was quickly apparent a miscalculation had been made. When the fog rolled in, Sergeant Maloney started firing the gun (less cannon ball). Every half hour he touched off the old gun, sending a powerful boom echoing out into the gray darkness. After two months of "fog bombarding," he explained the problem in a letter to the district superintendent. "I cannot find any person here to relieve me, not five minutes; I have been up three days and nights, had only two hours rest. I was nearly used up. All the rest I would require in twenty-four is two, if only I could get it." Responding to the plea, the superintendent did eventually provide some help for the beleaguered artillerist.

The isolation at Point Bonita was a difficult problem to overcome and essentially it never was solved. After a while the hardworking Sergeant Maloney quit, as did seven other keepers during a nine-month period in 1855-56! One keeper complained, "There are no inhabitants within five miles of this point, from San Francisco to Point Bonita; there is no direct communication but by chance, a sailboat may be procured at an expense of $5, and from $2 to $5 per barrel for freight. My first assistant would only take the appointment by my agreeing to make our salaries equal, even then he would only remain four months."

The very topography was inhospitable. One keeper was so fearful of his children falling off the cliffs, he harnessed them and gave each a rope tether. If they fell, it would not be very far!

As experience with both the light and cannon was gained, and mariners provided their comments, it was obvious that there were significant problems. The light was frequently not seen and even the thundering of the big fog gun went unheard. A new mechanically-operated fog bell helped solve the sound problem, but the invisible light was still a problem.

The Point Bonita Lighthouse is set high on towering cliffs. The suspension bridge is in the background. U.S. Coast Guard photo.

The lighthouse was built on the highest point the engineers could find, some 300 feet above sea level. This was normal practice for the East Coast but was a poor choice for the Pacific where fogs often are very high. The surface of the sea could be completely clear, but several hundred feet higher the fog could hide everything in a grey shroud. In many cases this is exactly what happened and Point Bonita Light was thus invisible to sailors. The only solution was to lower the light. In reality this meant building an entirely new lighthouse closer to the water level. A location at the very tip of Point Bonita, known as "Land's End," was selected.

It was an extremely difficult spot on which to build. When the construction crew reached the site and looked firsthand at the actual location, many of the men refused to work. The towing cliffs and sliding rock made it too dangerous! To reach the construction site it was necessary to have both men and supplies hauled up sheer cliffs. Rock slides were commonplace. In the end though, the job was accomplished. The new lighthouse, complete with fog horn building, was finished. On February 2, 1877, the light was shown for the first time. Instead of building a new one, the Lighthouse Service actually moved the old lamproom and mated it to the new base. The resulting tower was 33 feet high with a focal plane 140 feet above the sea. They even built a landing platform and derrick for lifting supplies off boats and a small cable-operated railroad for hauling the heavy stores of coal needed for the steam-operated fog whistle. Later in the year, Chinese-American workers cut a 188-foot long tunnel from the mainland out to the lighthouse, eliminating the need to use a very narrow and dangerous path along the sheer cliffs. The new tunnel was just wide enough for a one-horse cart to haul supplies. Later a 155-foot-long suspension bridge was also built to make the trip to the light even easier.

A number of vessels wrecked on Point Bonita. In 1874 the tug *Rescue* hit the rocks, but quick action by the keepers saved eight of her nine-man crew. When the Point Bonita Life Saving Station opened in 1899, there was plenty of work.

The most notable rescue, however, was performed by Lightkeeper George D. Cobb. Point Bonita was lonely anytime, but perhaps on December 26, 1896, it was even worse. A gale was churning the sea and powerful waves smashing hard into the rocks below, sending cold shards of water high up the cliffs. While watching out to sea, Cobb saw a sailboat capsize, dumping it's three occupants into the sea! Cobb realized there was no time to call the life-savers. Action was needed now!

Cobb swiftly ran to the landing and released the station lifeboat from its steel davits. Alone, this was a very difficult job, trying both to lower the

The Point Bonita Lighthouse tower. U.S. Coast Guard photo.

heavy boat and control its wind-blown swinging. Once he had the boat it the water, he cast off the pelican hooks and rowed hard for the struggling men. Since the lifeboat was designed for two men to row, Cobb had a exhausting time, but persevered. Fighting both wind and wave, he worked his way skillfully past the surf crashing onto the offshore reefs, and reached the overturned boat. Two of the men were still alive but unconscious. With near superhuman strength he heaved them over the gunwhale and aboard.

Looking for the third man, he found him in among some rocks. He, too, was unconscious. Deftly, Cobb maneuvered the boat into the deadly rocks and dragged him aboard too. Cut by the sharp rocks, the third man was bleeding profusely. With both skill and strength, Cobb brought the boat back to the light and landed the men safely.

All of the men recovered and, in recognition of the single-handed rescue, Cobb received the Silver Life Saving Medal. It was a rare honor for the brave keeper! Very few lightkeepers received such a prestigious award.

Point Bonita has the distinction of being the last manned light station on the California coast. In 1981, the station was finally automated and transferred to the National Park Service and is now part of the Golden Gate National Recreation Area. For 125 years, lightkeepers like George Cobb braved the dangers of Point Bonita. There would be no more. Now it was only the forlorn cry of the gulls and perhaps a ghostly keeper or two still living on the point.

Regardless of the eventual disposition of Point Bonita Light, Cobb's rescuing days were far from over. After all his time at Point Bonita, one might surmise he had seen enough of fog, but apparently not. On the morning of December 14, 1916, the U.S. Submarine H-3, bound from Astoria, Washington, to Eureka, California, went ashore in a dense fog at Samoa Beach, California, four miles above the entrance to Humbolt Bay. Built only three years before, she was one of the newest ships in the Navy. When word of the incident reached the Coast Guard Station four miles to the south, a scratch rescue crew was assembled including Coast Guardsmen, volunteers from the U.S. Engineers' force, and George Cobb from the fog signal station. Using a two-horse team, the crew reached the beach opposite H-3 shortly after noon. The submarine lay broadside-to, about 200 yards out from shore and in the thick of the breaking surf. The seas were rolling completely over her and the submarine was rocking side to side with their impact. There was no sign of life other than an occasional mournful blast from her fog horn.

Using their Lyle gun, the rescuers promptly fired a shotline right over the submarine, but none of her 27-man crew would come on deck to take it. Fearing than the crew may be trapped inside the steel coffin, the Coast

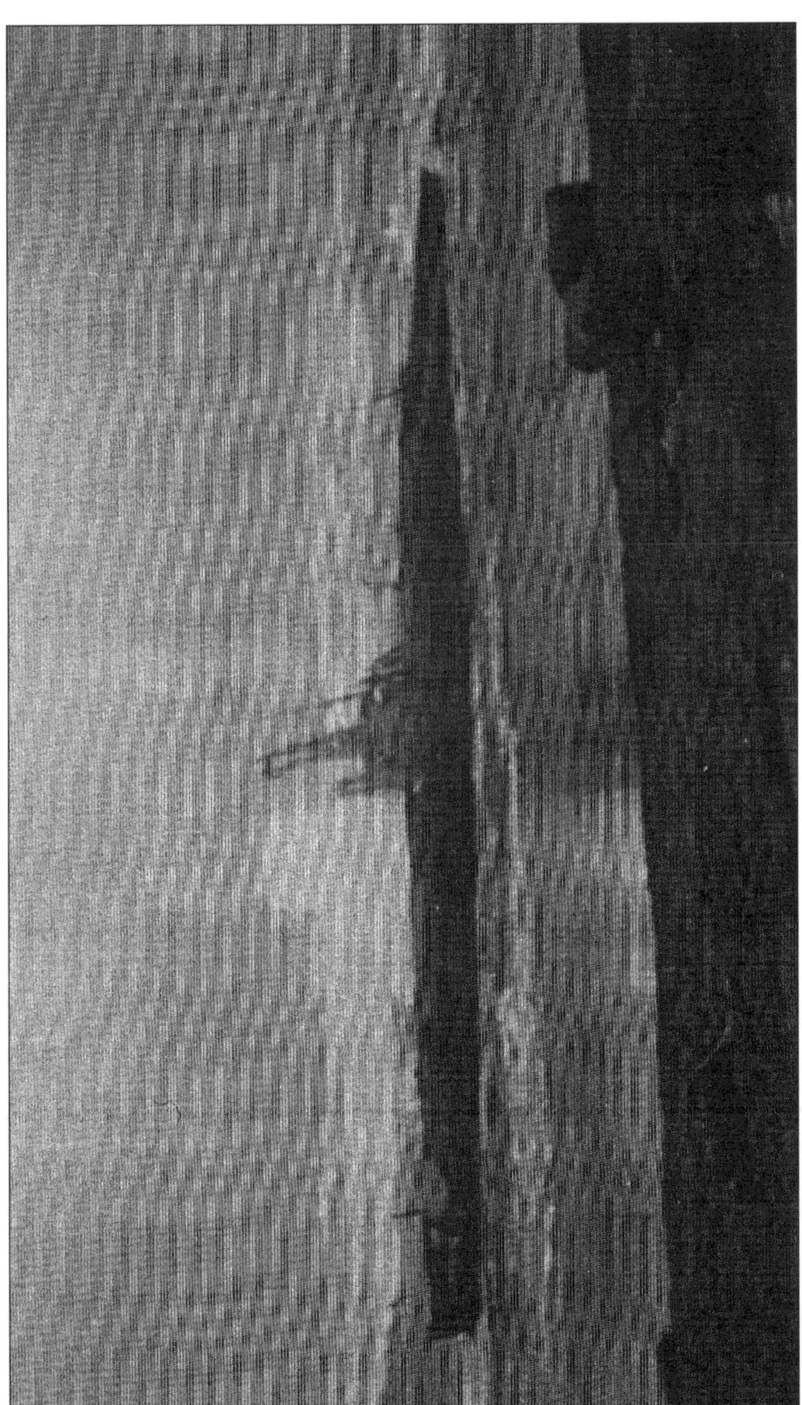

The submarine H-3 was trapped in the Pacific surf. National Archives photo.

Guardsmen returned to the station for their surfboat. If the submarine crew couldn't come out, the Coast Guard would have to go them! At 3:00 p.m., the tide ebbed and the surf moderated somewhat. The Coast Guard fired another line across the submarine. Now, some of the crew came up on deck, hauled in the shotline and made fast the tailblock and hawser but were unable to clear the gear. They abandoned their effort and fled back below. When the surfboat arrived on the beach a short time later, the Coast Guard crew rowed out through the breakers to the rocking submarine. The vessel was still rolling heavily and the light surfboat was unable to pull along side. One of the Coast Guardsmen volunteered to jump to the submarine. Timing his leap to the motion of the submarine, he leaped and safely reached the vessel. Holding onto the submarine with one hand, he quickly cleared the breeches buoy gear

The submarine H-3 was still firmly ashore. National Archives photo.

The crew of the Milwaukee *was safely brought ashore by the Coast Guard. National Archives photo.*

with the other. By this time a large crowd of several hundred people had gathered on shore to watch the odd shipwreck. Although they wanted to help, they were difficult to control and in the confusion, one of the crowd made the hawser fast to a tree stump. When the submarine rolled, the strain on the rope was too great and it snapped. As the whipline was still intact, another hawser was quickly sent out and the breeches buoy again established. All aboard the submarine were safely brought ashore. Lightkeeper George Cobb was a critical part of the rescue team and its eventual success was, in measure, due to his efforts. Rescuing the submarine's crew was surely a unique episode in the annals of lightkeeping.

Cobb's involvement in the H-3 wreck was over, but the drama for the Navy was just beginning. Between December 15-20, ineffective efforts to free the submarine were made by the Coast Guard cutter *McCulloch*, U.S. Monitor *Cheyenne,* and Navy tug *Arapahoe*. The Navy then requested bids from private concerns to salvage the submarine. The resulting bids were considered too high, so the Navy decide to do the job itself. Deciding that it was just a case of more power, the Navy brought in the heavy cruiser *Milwaukee* with her 24,504-horsepower. The Navy ran a heavy hawser between the *Milwaukee* and the 1,000-horsepower Navy tug *Iroquois,* and another from the *Milwaukee* to the H-3. On command, the two ships went full ahead. Surely, their brute force would pull the submarine free. The pulling hawsers grew tighter and tighter and finally the one between the *Milwaukee* and *Iroquois* snapped, sending the cruiser veering off to starboard and hard aground in the breakers!

The Coast Guard and their trusty old beach cart returned to the H-3 wreck and went to work. Over the next two days they removed 150 of the crew by breeches buoy and the rest by surfboat. Not a single life was lost.

The H-3 was finally salvaged when a commercial contractor put her on large log rollers and took her over land to Humbolt Bay. She was repaired and returned to service. In 1931 she was finally scraped. The *Milwaukee* was not so lucky. She was a hopeless loss, to the great embarrassment of the Navy.[1]

Footnotes

1. *Annual Report of the Commissioner of Lighthouses 1917* (Washington, DC: Government Printing Office, 1917); *Annual Report of the U.S. Coast Guard*, 1916, Washington, DC: Government Printing Office; "Clipping File," RG 26, NARA; James A. Gibbs, *Sentinels of the North Pacific* (Portland, Oregon: Binfords and Mort, 1955), pp. 43-45; "Journal of the Light Station

at Humbolt Bay Fog Signal," December 1916, NARA; *Lighthouse Service Bulletin,* February 1, 1917; "Naming File," U.S. Coast Guard Historian's Office; Navy Department, Dictionary of American Naval Fighting Ships, Volume III (Naval History Division, 1967), pp. 196-197; Ralph Shanks and Lisa Woo Shanks, Editor, *Guardians of the Golden Gate* (Petaluma, California: Costano Books, 1990), pp. 65-103.

XIII
William James Tate
Into The Wild Blue Yonder

Some lightkeepers have been involved in the leading edge of lighthouse technology, such as experimenting with new lenses and fuels. But William Tate was part of an entirely new endeavor–aviation! During the earliest experiments the Wright Brothers conducted at Kitty Hawk, North Carolina, during the 1900-1903 period, Tate provided invaluable assistance.

The Tate family came to the Outer Banks of North Carolina in a time-honored method. According to local legend, Bill's father was a shipwreck victim who decided to stay and take up residence. Bill's father, William Douglas Tate, was captain of the clipper ship B.M. *Prescott*, bound from Boston to San Francisco via Cape Horn, when she was driven ashore off Kitty Hawk in March, 1849. His brother, Dan, was the mate. The two men survived the disaster, helped to the beach by several natives. Apparently the two bedraggled sailors liked what they saw and decided to settle on the lonely and desolate Outer Banks. The two men were well-educated and set up a grocery store as well as a weekly freight and passenger boat run from Kitty Hawk to Elizabeth City.

Bill Tate had a difficult early life. Born in 1869, his mother died when he was eight. Three years later his father was on his way back to Kitty Hawk from Currituck Courthouse on the mainland when his boat capsized in rough water. The elder Tate managed to lash himself to the hull, but by the time it drifted ashore, he had frozen to death. Bill then lived with his uncle, Dan, a storekeeper, for two years before being sent to the Masonic orphanage on the mainland for four years. Later he graduated from the Atlantic Collegiate Institute in Elizabeth City, North Carolina. For a "Banker," he had received a very good education. When he returned to Kitty Hawk, he worked as a clerk for his uncle Dan until Dan's death, when he took over the business. When the original store burned, he built a new one combining store, living quarters and Post Office. Tate eventually became a county commissioner, notary public, fisherman and postmaster. He was the classic example of a self-made man.

Tate married Addie Sibbern, the daughter of the man who rescued his father and uncle from the surf. It was reported that when Tate asked Addie's father for her hand the father said, "I should have let them Tates (William and Daniel) drown in the ocean at Kitty Hawk, then William's son wouldn't be here asking to marry my daughter."

His involvement with aviation began simply enough. The Wrights were looking for a location that had both adequate space and weather conditions for their experiments. The first inquiry letters concerning Kitty Hawk were simply addressed to the local postmaster.[1] Bill took the time to answer the letter with a very encouraging reply. "You would find here nearly any type of ground you could wish; you could for instance, get a stretch of sandy land one mile by five miles with a bare hill in the center 80 feet high, not a tree or bush anywhere to break the evenness of the wind current. This in my opinion would be a fine place: our winds are always steady, generally from 10 to 20 miles velocity per hour …if you decide to try your machine here & come I will take pleasure in doing all I can for your convenience & success & pleasure & I assure you you will find a hospitable people when you come among us."

At the time he wrote to the Wrights, he was not connected with the Lighthouse Service. Carefully considering Tate's information, the Wrights decided to go to Kitty Hawk. The Wrights were sold on the virtues of the Outer Banks. Kitty Hawk was a very remote and inaccessible location, which allowed the brothers to work without the glare of publicity. On September 12, 1900, the Wrights arrived, but only after a three day trip on a "miserable little flat-bottomed schooner"–named the *Curlicue*. When they arrived at Tate's home they had not eaten for two days! During this first trip the pioneer aviators boarded with Tate and his wife and became good friends with his family. The Wrights were well satisfied with their first year's gliding experiments.

Twenty-five years after the first successful flight, Tate remembered, "The mental attitude of the natives toward the Wrights was that they were a simple pair of harmless cranks that were wasting their time at a fool attempt to do something that was impossible. The chief argument against their success could be heard at the stores and post office and ran something like this: 'God didn't intend man to fly. If He did, He would have given him a set of wings on his shoulders. No, siree, nobody need not try to do what God didn't intend for him to do.' I recall, not once, but many times, that when I cited the fact that other things as wonderful had been accomplished, I was quickly told that I was a 'Darned sight crazier than the Wrights were.'"

The first experimental glider was assembled in Tate's yard in 1900. On November 27, 1927, Orville wrote to Tate reminding him that "All of the parts were built in Dayton and shipped to Kitty Hawk, excepting four spars which were made and shipped in from Norfolk. The ribs, struts, hinges and end bows were all built complete at our shop in Dayton. The wing coverings were also cut and sewed in Dayton, but on account of Wilbur's inability to get 20-foot spars at Norfolk, a change was necessary in the coverings. I remember he said this work was done on Mrs. Tate's sewing machine."

Tom Tate, the young son of Bill's uncle Dan, was a frequent and enthusiastic visitor to the Wright's experiments. Because the gliders weren't big enough to carry a man, Tom was given some thrilling rides! Dan also worked as a handyman for the Wrights.

In another letter, Orville recalled how much Tate knew of the early flying machines. "I do not think the Department of Justice would expect you to know as much about our other machines as you do about the first one, because you saw more of the first one. As I remember, when we came back to Kitty Hawk in 1901, Irene and Pauline were wearing dresses made from the sateen wing coverings of our first machine."

Tate frequently assisted in launching and recovering the glider and in many of the experiments in 1900. Testing the gliders was exhausting work. In 1901, the Wrights made 50-100 glides and in 1902, 700-1,000! Their best record for time in the air was a short one minute and 12 seconds. Considering that after each flight the glider had to be laboriously hauled back up to the top of the hill over loose sand, it was indeed hard work. On May 2, 1928, a commemorative marker, paid for by the citizens of Kitty Hawk, was built on the exact spot in his yard where the first glider was set up. After the initial shock of the flyers from Dayton, the local people accepted them with open arms. Tate wrote, "Ask any person who knew them and you will be told that they were the two of the finest men that ever honored our community with their presence. Their uniform disposition of holding themselves aloof and above the ordinary man, as well as their disposition always at all times to be ready to render every courtesy to everyone, no matter how humble or unlettered, endeared these men to our coast people forever. Proud fathers have named their sons after them and the names Wilbur and Orville will endure forever on our section of the North Carolina coast."

In spite of all his early work with the Wrights, Bill was not present on that fateful December 17, 1903, when the first powered flight occurred. At the time, he was living six miles away from Kill Devil Hill and was only infrequently able to be present as the Wrights grew closer and closer to the time for flight. The Wrights thought highly enough of him, however, to let him know that they planned to try a powered flight on December 17, and told him to be present for the occasion. When Bill got up that morning, he immediately checked the weather. The wind was gusting and temperature hovering around freezing. He couldn't believe the Wrights would try on such a day, so he saved himself a long horseback ride and stayed home. Later he reconsidered and headed south for Kitty Hawk. As he reached the Kitty Hawk Post Office, one of the local lifesaving station crew ran up the beach and shouted, "They have done it! They have done it! Damned if it ain't flew!" Bill had missed the preeminent event in aviation history! At 10:35 a.m., Wilbur Wright flew 120 feet in 12 seconds. He had forever shattered the bond that kept man glued to the earth. As time passed, Tate came to regard missing the flight as "the greatest regret of my life." After all, it was solely due to his help that the Wrights were even at the Outer Banks.

Tate stayed at Kitty Hawk until 1913, when he moved to Norfolk, Virginia, so his two daughters could attend high school. A good education had always been important in the Tate family. He took a job as a raft inspector for the U.S. Corps of Engineers. On July 1, 1915, he transferred to the Lighthouse Service and was stationed at Long Point, North Carolina. This job required him to care for 14 light beacons on the inland waterway from Blackwater River to North River Bar. Every 30 days all had to be charged with gas, the lens and burners cleaned, and structures painted and kept in good order. He stayed on the job until 1922, when the station was moved to Coinjock, North Carolina. Tate retired in 1940, at age 70.

Over the years Tate kept up his friendship with the Wrights and his interest in aviation. In 1920, he was the first lighthouse keeper to make an aerial inspection on navigational lights by airplane, with his aviator son-in-law. He later reported, "This keeper made the trip along the river in an airplane, flying about on a level with the lights and within 50 feet of the same, and it was easily seen whether they were burning." As lightkeeper he rendered assistance to disabled airplanes several times.

Tate was often honored for his early role in helping the Wrights. In December 1937, he was a guest of honor at the annual dinner of the Aero

The 1901 glider being launched with William and Dan Tate assisting at the Wing tips. National Archives photo.

Postmaster William Tate and family. National Archives photo.

Club in Washington, DC, commemorating the 34th anniversary of the first powered flight. Later the same year he was the guest of Henry and Edsel Ford at Dearborn, Michigan during an affair celebrating Orville's seventy-first birthday.

While keeper at North Carolina's North Landing Light on Currituck Sound, at the entrance to the Albemarle and Chesapeake Canal, Tate assisted many craft in trouble. Although not the spectacular rescues of other keepers, they do demonstrate the type of help keepers often provided, as well as his dedication and ingenuity.

The William Tate *hits the river. Marinette Marine Corporation photo.*

July 16, 1916–Rescued a man in a launch in trouble near the station.
July 28, 1916–Rendered valuable assistance in refloating the schooner *Hobson*
September 6, 1916–Floated the gasoline freighter *R. C. Beaman*
September 7, 1916–Floated *Muriel Dean* and repaired disabled motorboat
September 25, 1916–Again floated the *R. C. Beaman*
January 2-26, 1917–Rendered assistance to four men, one woman and an infant from a disabled aircraft, sheltered them at the light station and repaired the aircraft.
January 9, 1917–Assisted party in disabled motorboat
March 19, 1917–Towed a disabled motorboat to harbor
March 27, 1917–Assisted grounded state fisheries boat
November 23, 1917–Piloted lost yacht *Ildewell* to a safe harbor
November 30, 1917–Floated stranded yacht, repaired disable yacht *Abeola*
1919–Assisted disabled launch
1921–Floated submarine chaser aground near light
1921–Towed barge with rescued crew of burned tugboat to safety
1922–Assisted grounded yacht *Linnie*
1922–Floated two submarine chasers aground near light
1923–Floated yacht *Aimee*, ashore near station

Tate died at Coinjock on June 8, 1953, and is buried in the Baum Cemetery at Kitty Hawk. From whale oil lamps to powered flight, Lightkeeper William J. Tate had seen it all. He had also helped to make history.[2]

Footnotes

1. There is some dispute whether it was Bill or his wife who was the actual postmaster.

2. *Annual Report of the Commissioner of Lighthouses*, 1916, 1917, 1919, 1921, 1922, 1923, Hans Christian Adamson, *Keepers of the Lights* (New York: Greenberg, 1967), pp. 158-160; Interview, Suzanne Tate, August 12, 1999; *Lighthouse Service Bulletin*, January 1, September 1, November 1, 1916, April 2, May 1, 1917, January 2, March 1938; *Light List, Atlantic and Gulf Coasts of the United States, 1915* (Washington: Government Printing Office, 1915), p. 196; "Naming File," U.S. Coast Guard Historian's Office.

XIV
Marcus Hanna
Above And Beyond

Receiving a medal for heroism is a very rare thing. Receiving two is rarer still. Only once was a Congressional Medal of Honor and a Gold Lifesaving Medal awarded to the same recipient and that was Marcus Hanna, a man of truly remarkable courage.

His parents, James and Eliza, were lightkeepers on Franklin Island, Maine. Because of the remoteness of the lighthouse, Eliza went home to Bristol, Maine, to have her child and it was there Marcus was born on November 3, 1842.

For the first 10 years of his life, he lived at his father's lighthouse. Franklin Island was a lonely and forsaken place. Many vessels were wrecked in the locale due to the treacherous reefs and shoals. Doubtless while he was there, he learned responsibility and the rudiments of good seamanship. He never completed a formal education and at age 10 went to sea, as was common for boys of the Pine Tree State. By a age 18, he had worked his way up to being a ship's steward on a packet running between Gloucester, Massachusetts, and New York City.

When the Civil War started, Marcus joined the Navy, serving on the U.S.S. *Ohio*, U.S.S. *Mississippi* and U.S.S. *Niagara* of the Gulf Squadron. During this period he participated in actions against rebel gunboats on the Mississippi River. After a year of service, he mustered out in Boston.

Marcus returned to Maine where attempted to enlist with a volunteer unit, but when it became evident that the unit would not see service, he went to

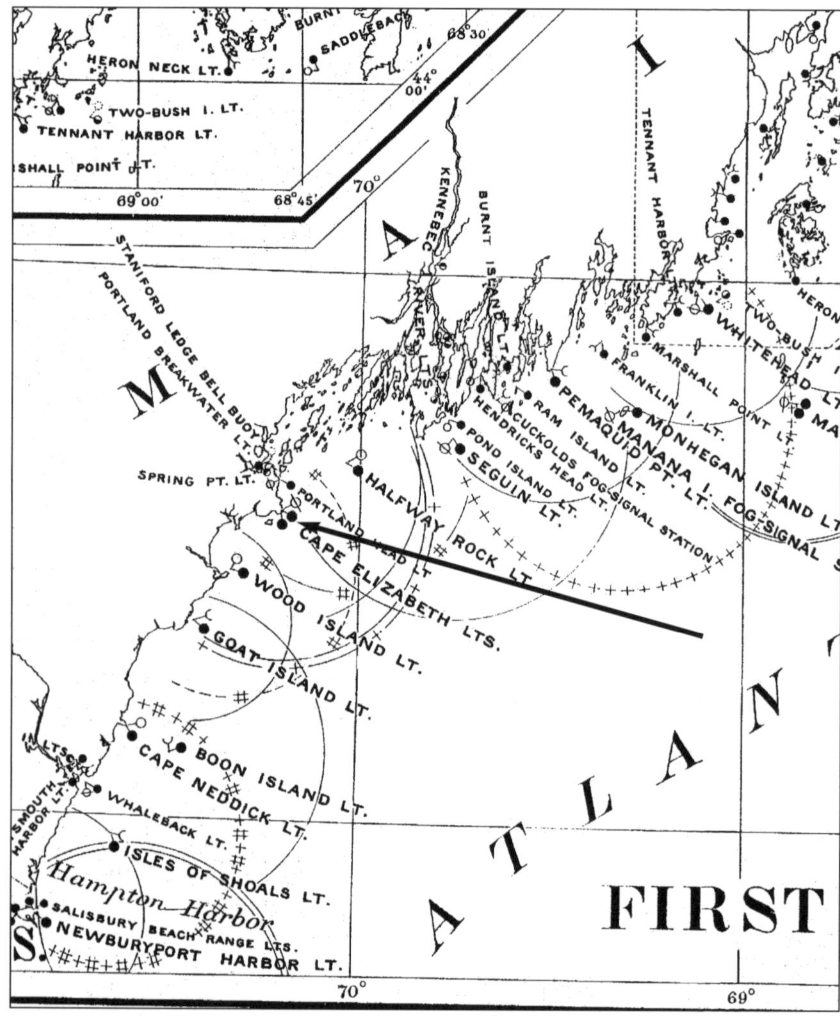

Rockland, Massachusetts, where he joined Company B, 50th Volunteer Infantry. This unit was later assigned to the siege of Port Hudson, Louisiana. During this operation, dysentery and malaria were widespread, and Marcus contracted a malarial infection that plagued him for the rest of his life.

The battle heated up for Marcus on July 4, 1863. His company was given picket duty in support of an Illinois artillery battery and positioned in shallow rifle pits, a mere 150 yards from the Port Hudson fortifications. The position was periodically swept by musket fire as the rebels replied to the cannonading. The day was terrifically hot and humid and by noon the men had exhausted their water supplies and were beginning to drop from heat

Marcus Hanna

exhaustion. When an officer called for a volunteer to go back for water, involving moving over a half-mile of open terrain, Marcus, by then a sergeant, volunteered.

Loaded with 10 or 12 canteens, Marcus was up and out of the trenches "like a rabbit," dodging across the open landscape. A hail of musket fire erupted from the rebel fortifications, but he was not hit. After proceeding to the water hole, he returned to his comrades. Although the rebels, seeing he was carrying water, did not try as hard to hit him, he was still under fire on the return trip. The only wound Marcus received was a stray pellet in his calf. After the conclusion of the Port Hudson campaign, the 50th Volunteers were returned to Boston and mustered out of Federal Service.

Marcus had not had enough of soldiering and on September 10, 1863, enlisted as a sergeant with the 2nd Massachusetts Heavy Artillery which served as a garrison unit in North Carolina. He remained with this unit until the end of the war, the last nine months as a Second lieutenant.

Although the medal was not awarded until November 2, 1895, thirty-two years later, the citation recalled clearly the action on that desperate day so long ago! Sergeant Marcus Hanna "voluntarily exposed himself to heavy fire to get water for comrades in the rifle pits."[1]

Three months after mustering out, Marcus married Louisana Davis of Bristol, Maine. The next four years of his life were spend piloting a small vessel supplying a fish market. In July of 1869, he was appointed keeper at the Pemaquid Lighthouse. During the winter months, Marcus and Louisiana worked as teachers at the local school.

Marcus transferred to the twin towers at Cape Elizabeth Light outside of Portland, Maine. The light marked the southern bank of the tricky channel into Portland Harbor and was considered an important station. The original towers were built in 1828. Cheaply made of rubble, they lacked the size and strength required of important seacoast lights. In 1873, the towers were torn down and replaced with two cast iron towers, 300 yards apart. A new fog whistle was also built. A new second order Fresnel was installed in the East Tower in 1884 and keeper Hanna was the first to use it.

Marcus's Gold Lifesaving Medal was awarded as the result of the wreck of the schooner *Australia* on January 28, 1885. The story is best related directly from the pages of the *Annual Report of the U. S. Life Saving Service*.

> It appears from the evidence presented to the Department that the schooner *Australia*, of Booth Bay, Maine, having a crew of three men, viz., J. W. Lewis, master, and Irving Pierce and William Kellar, seamen, left her home port on January 27, 1885, laden with fish and guano, for

Cape Elizabeth Light.

Cape Elizabeth Light. U.S. Coast Guard photo.

Boston, Mass. At about midnight a furious gale and snowstorm set in. After losing some of her sails, she attempted to reach Portland Harbor, but making the land to leeward, was driven onto the rocks at Cape Elizabeth, near the fog-signal, just to the westward of Dyer's Point. She struck just after 8 o'clock the morning of the 28th. The seas now poured over her in a perfect deluge, sweeping away everything about decks, including the house, the men having barely time to take to the rigging. Even there it was not safe, for in a few moments the captain was washed away and drowned. The sufferings of the other two, drenched to the skin and with the temperatures at 10 degrees below zero, were terrible. The masts of the vessel were soon afterwards discovered through the driving snow by Mrs. Hanna, the wife of the light-keeper. The latter had lain down for a nap upon being relieved at the fog signal soon after daylight by one of his assistants, Hiram Staples. His wife's explanation of alarm upon seeing the wreck was sufficient to arouse Hanna and slipping on his coat, hat and boots, he rushed down to the shore. Upon

Left: Gold Lifesaving Medal. Author's photo. Right: Medal of Honor. U.S. Coast Guard photo.

reaching the fog signal he called to Staple to follow and the two were soon abreast of the wreck. Two men could be seen in the rigging, who at once began shouting for help. Hanna knew it was impossible to launch a boat, but his mind was soon made up. He returned to the fog signal for an axe and then hastened to a boat house three hundred yards distant for a line with which to rescue the men. Finding the door blocked by a great mass of snow, he ran back, shouting to Staples, who had remained in the fog-signal to bring a shovel, quick! An entrance was soon effected with the axe and a suitable line obtained. Meanwhile, Mrs. Hanna had alarmed the families at the station, only one member of which, however, Mr. Staples son, a lad of fifteen, could render any help. Hanna dispatched him to summon the neighbors and then got down to his work. Weighting one end of the line with a piece of metal obtained from the signal-house, so he could more readily throw it, he clambered down the slippery, ice-coated rocks, almost into the surf and attempted to heave it on board. His situation while thus engaged was one of almost as great peril as that of the two men in the rigging of the schooner. The slightest misstep would have been fatal. The brave fellow had been ill for a week or more and it was only through the exercise of a most determined will that he was able to stand the hardships and exposure and maintain his footing. After many unsuccessful efforts to reach the men with the line, which fell short, he was compelled to crawl back on to the level ground to restore warmth by beating and stamping his almost frozen hands and feet. He also improved the opportunity to free the stiffened lined of its coating of ice. His assistant, Staples, also suffering intensely with the cold, and discouraged by Hanna's ill success, had meanwhile retreated to the signal-house to warm himself, leaving the keeper alone. At about this time a tremendous wave lifted the schooner bodily and threw her on her beam-ends, thus placing the two men in greater peril than before. Filled with dismay at this, Hanna again descended over the rocks in the face of the blinding, drenching spray and summoning all of his remaining strengths succeeded, after several failures, in at last reaching the schooner with the line. One of the men, Pierce, adjusted it around his body and while he was doing so Hanna crawled back on to the bank and shouted for aid. No response came for not a soul was in sight. As soon as he was ready, Pierce made signal to the keeper and casting himself into the ice breakers, he was with difficulty, drawn out on the shore. The man's jaws were set and he appeared almost gone. Realizing that every moment was precious, Hanna quickly loosened the line from Pierce's body and after a few more efforts, threw it within Kellar's grasp. The process was then repeated as it Pierce's case and Kellar was nearly ashore when, to the keeper's great relief, Staples and two of the neighbors came hurrying to his assistance. The rest of the story is soon told. The two sailors were carried into the fog-signal building, where their frozen garments were removed and every possible means resorted to for their restoration. They were both badly frostbitten, but as the storm continued with great violence all day and the snow was drifting badly, it was impossible to remove them to the more comfortable dwelling of the keeper, a few hundred yards away, until the following morning. There they were tenderly nursed by Hanna and his wife until the roads could be opened and communication had with the city, when the poor fellows were carried to the marine hospital in Portland for treatment, where they soon came around all right. That these men would have shared the fate of the captain but for the self-sacrificing devotion of the brave keeper is beyond doubt. His noble conduct was held deserving of the highest form of recognition within the power of the Service to bestow. The captain's body was recovered subsequently.[2]

She's in! The Marcus Hanna *hits the river. Marinette Marine Corporation photo.*

Marcus Hanna died on December 12, 1921, and was buried at Portland Head Cemetery. He was 79 years old. His wife, Louisiana, died in 1936 and was buried next to him. So ended the tale of a remarkable hero of the old Lighthouse Service.

The lighthouse at Cape Elizabeth also saw a lightkeeping tragedy. Late one night in 1934, the wife of keeper Joseph H. Upton woke to find he had not returned from the tower. Running out to the tower, she found him lying unconscious as the bottom of the tower stairs. Rushed to a Portland hospital, he died of a fractured skull. The lighthouse was automated in 1963.[3]

Footnotes

1. "Medal of Honor Citations," [http://www.army.mil/cmh-pg/mohciv.htm].

2. *Annual Report, U.S. Life Saving Service* (Washington, DC: Government Printing Office, 1885) pp. 40-42.

3. "Cape Elizabeth Light to Change," [http://www.1hdigest.com/archives/1998/sept98/Capeliz.htm]; "Clipping File," RG 26, NARA; "Naming File," U.S. Coast Guard Historian's Office;

XV
Harry Claiborne
Hurricane Again!

Hurricanes were and are a way of life for lightkeepers along the Atlantic and Gulf Coasts of the United States. In point of fact, the English language is unable to fully express the awesome power of these storms. Simply defining it as a "...cyclonic storm which blows with a velocity of from 63 knots to 118 knots but rarely over..." does not even begin to describe their immense destructive power.

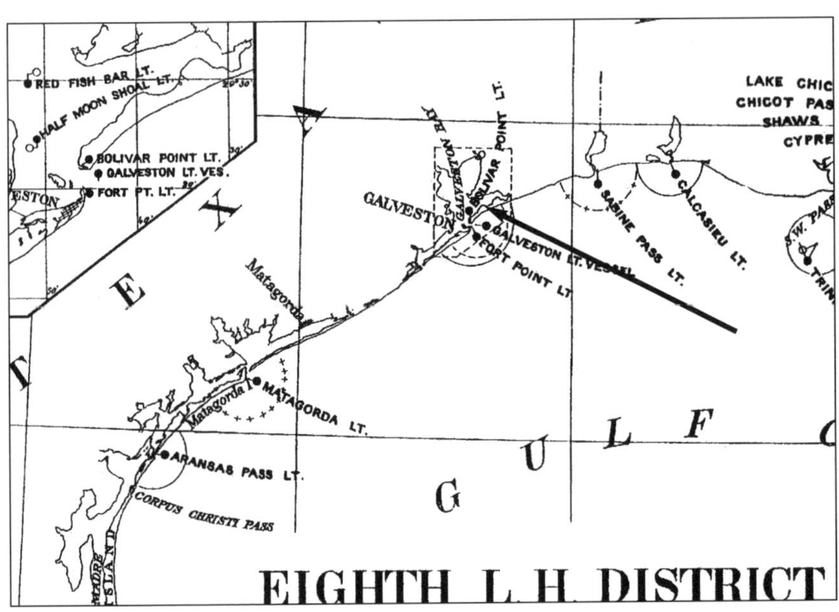

Keeper Harry C. Claiborne, keeper of the Bolivar Point Light off Galveston, Texas, experienced two of the most potent hurricanes on record. During both of them he not only provided shelter for townspeople at his light, but also, kept his light burning.

Claiborne was born in New Orleans in 1859, in the midst of the hustle and bustle of the city known as the "Queen of the South." The Mississippi was the highway into the riches of America's heartland and from the New Orleans terminus, the goods were shipped around the world. Why Claiborne became a lightkeeper isn't known, but in June of 1887, at the age of 28, he was appointed as the second assistant keeper of the South West Pass Light below New Orleans, at a salary of $325 yearly. Before the Mississippi reached the open sea, it divided into three branches. Each was commonly called a "pass." Clairborne's South West Pass was the most westerly branch and the second busiest of the three. Day after day, long lines of ships passed the lighthouse. In spite of the nearby ship traffic, the lighthouse was a lonely place built on a large area of swamp. At high tide the entire station grounds were flooded, which meant every building had to be built on stilts and interconnected with boardwalks.

In the summer of 1889, Claiborne was appointed as the keeper of the Pass a l'Outre Lighthouse, marking the eastern entrance to the Mississippi from the Gulf of Mexico. Like his previous station, it, too, was built on marshland requiring all buildings to be on stilts with connecting boardwalks. Every year the buildings sank a little bit deeper into the swamp, necessitating jacking them all back up. Even the light tower sank, so the door had to be raised every year. In the mid-1800s this was also the busiest pass. During the Civil War it was a key position for the Union forces in their campaign to capture New Orleans. Rebels would infiltrate down the Mississippi and extinguish the light in an effort to cause Union ships to run aground. After the war, a large sandbar formed in the pass, preventing large ships from using the waterway. Since the government had just dredged the South Pass, there was no reason the spend money doing it in Pass a l'Outre and few ships used it. As a result, it was a bleak place for a lightkeeper. One inspector noted in a report that it was "...one of the loneliest stations I ever visited, as no vessel even passes and the nearest neighbor is sixteen miles away." Yellow fever and malaria were common. The only advantage the station offered Claiborne was the increase in pay, from $325 yearly as an assistant to $680 as a keeper.

When the keeper's job at Bolivar Point in Texas opened in 1895, Claiborne jumped at it. He quickly moved his family to the light and settled in. Even though he took a $40 pay cut to transfer to Bolivar Point, it was infinitely better than the dismal light at Pass a l'Outre.

Bolivar Point Light, circa 1920. U.S. Coast Guard photo.

Bolivar Point Light was located at the tip of a long peninsula across the bay from Galveston. The city was on the east end of a low sand island, about 30 miles long and one-half to three miles wide. Bolivar Point was to the northeast of Galveston. It was a 20 mile-long sand spit varying in width from one-quarter to three miles wide. There were few people on the peninsula but in comparison with his previous light, it was a veritable metropolis! Once a month he or his assistant had to row across the bay to Galveston for supplies. Life at the lighthouse was generally very quiet. Mrs. Claiborne once wrote in a letter that "life ...was very lonely and friendless. There is very little visiting because travel is non-existent from the point to Galveston. We pass most of our time reading books."

The first light from the Bolivar Lighthouse was exhibited on November 19, 1872. The 117-foot-high tower was made of brick sheathed in heavy cast-iron plates bolted tightly together. The light was actually ready to be exhibited by the end of October, but a delay in receiving the lantern glass kept the tower dark. Both the tower and small keeper's dwelling were surrounded by a white picket fence, adding a homey touch to a very austere environment. The tower and its second order Fresnel, guided sailors until 1933, when it was replaced by a new light at the South Jetty.

The hurricane that struck on September 8, 1900, arrived without the typical warning residents were used to seeing. Hurricanes were not uncommon and people were used to seeing a "brick-dust sky" heralding their arrival. In the early afternoon of the 8th, weather observers even recorded seeing dabs of blue sky. Around noon, the heavy rain began. Initially, the wind was out of the north, veering between northwest and northeast. By early evening it had swung to the east, and just before midnight south or southwest. Storm velocity was reached about 1:00 p.m. and increased to hurricane force at 5:00 p.m. At 6:15 p.m. it screamed at 100 miles per hour and the weather station anemometer blew away! Three hours later, the government weather observer estimated it at over 120 miles per hour! Driven by the wind, flood water reached a height of 14 feet over low water, drowning the city under five feet at street level. After 11:00 p.m. it slowly decreased until it was a mere 26 miles per hour at 8:00 a.m. on September 9. Those are the "facts" of the storm.

Before the hurricane hit, Galveston was a city of some "...38,000 happy and busy people; a city of splendid homes and broad clean streets; a city of oleanders and roses and palms; a city of the finest churches, school buildings and benevolent institutions in the south; a thriving port with many ocean-going ships at anchor...; a sea side resort, with hundreds of bathers at play in the safest and most delightful surf in the world."[1]

After the hurricane–[it was a city of]

> ...32,000 stunned and stricken people, a thousand naked, five thousand bruised, ten thousand homeless, all searching for their friends among the slain, tearless but bleeding at the heart, unappalled and uncomplaining, a city of wrecked homes and streets choked with debris sandwiched with six thousand corpses; a city leafless and bloomless, with the slime of the ocean on every spot and in every house, a city with only three churches standing, not a school building or benevolent institution habitable; a port with shipping stranded and wrecked many miles from their moorings ...ocean going vessels sent crashing through railroad bridges or driven high onto the shore and shallow ...with not a timber of three thousand houses left to mark their sites; ...a city without lights except tallow candles and kerosene lamps; a city without freshwater except the slender store in a few up-ground cisterns; a city with food for scarcely a week.... This was Galveston on September 9, 1900, the sad and fateful Sunday when she awakened to her sorrow, when there was no preaching or public service, but when every soul had faced its God and knew its own accounting.[2]

Another account had this to say: "A full month after the storm in was not unusual to discover in the debris the remains of a stout boy with his right arm shattered and his left grasping the body of his baby brother: an emaciated dog guarding the corpse of his master stowed in a cavity in the wreckage; women with infants lashed to their backs..."[3]

There were few areas of safe refuge from the raw power of the terrible hurricane. Bolivar Light was such an oasis. During the height of the hurricane, Claiborne sheltered an estimated 125 men, women and children in the light tower.

When the fury of the storm started to escalate, people began arriving at the light. First it was nine men and two women who deserted a stranded passenger train. Fearing the train would be soon overwhelmed by the surging water, they ran through the grasping, gusts of wind, to the tower for safety. As the violence of the wind increased, other refugees arrived, fleeing not only the violence of the hurricane, but also the steadily rising water that was sweeping over the Boliver Peninsula. When Claiborne could see no more refugees heading for the tower, he slammed the heavy steel door shut and bolted it securely, locking out the violence of the storm.

The only place he could put the refugees was on the stairs that wound their way around and around until they ended at the lamp room. The people were packed tight as sardines, sitting two to a step! Where ever the refugees ended up was where they had to stay. They couldn't climb any higher and several feet of water flooded the bottom of the tower. They were sealed tight in a spiraling tunnel of darkness. All they could do was wait for the hurricane to die, or just storm along on its way. There was no food and what little water was available was given to the children. In a desperate effort to get more water, volunteers crawled out onto the narrow galley circling the lamp room to try to catch rain water in buckets. The first buckets of water were undrinkable. Even 130 feet above the ground, the driving rain was contaminated with salt! Later, as the wind slowly dropped, the volunteers were able to collect drinkable water which was passed to the thirsty refugees on the stairs.

When the water around the light finally dropped enough for the refugees to move and the door to the tower pushed open, a gristly discovery was made. A dozen bodies floated around the base, people who had reached the tower but in the screaming wind and surging waves, were apparently unable to get the attention of those within. If they pounded on the door, in the wild thunder of the storm they were not heard! Within mere feet of safety, they perished. Many of the living fell to the ground in prayer.

The lighthouse inspector for the district later wrote of Claiborne that "…the lives of one hundred and twenty-five people were saved and to my personal knowledge he harbored and fed a large number of them for a considerable period." Claiborne had just purchased a month's food for himself and family before the hurricane hit and all of it was consumed by his unexpected guests. He gave them clothing, bedding and literally all that he owned until everything was gone. He also lost virtually all of his personal property in the storm. Since his property was "…not being needed at the light-station for light-house purposes," it could not be claimed for reimbursement. Claiborne had his tower but, little more.

The lighthouse survived the hurricane relatively unscathed, considering the virtual destruction of Galveston. Repairs to the light ran through 1901, and much was done by hired labor under the supervision of Claiborne. Contract prices were considered too high by the Lighthouse Service for an acceptable bid. Since Galveston was, for practical purposes, completely destroyed, and labor for anything was at an absolute premium, the high price for contractors was understandable.

In 1909, the illumination was converted to incandescent oil vapor, the first and for a time, only such lighthouse in the Gulf. In all other respects, Claiborne's life was without notable incident.

Bolivar's quiet time ended on August 16, 1915, when another massive hurricane smashed into the Gulf. The storm started near Dominica in the Leeward Islands on August 10. Messages regarding its direction and location

The 1900 hurricane devastated Galveston. U.S. Coast Guard photo.

as the storm approached were of great value in preparing all of the communities in its path. Unlike the 1900 hurricane, the sky turned copper-colored on the morning of the 15th, giving clear indication of its approach. The wind started in puffs from the north before veering clockwise to the south as the storm bore steadily in. Wind speeds topped 120 miles per hour and nearly 15 1/2 inches of rain flooded the city.

The *Lighthouse Service Bulletin* of October 1915 described the hurricane's impact.

> Bolivar Light, since then [the September storm, 1900], has weathered another and a wilder night with the same keeper in charge and more storm tales have been woven into the history of the great beacon that stands at the entrance to Galveston Harbor.
>
> Sixty people, a large part of whom were women and children, spent the night of the recent Texas coast storm huddled on the circular stairs inside the lighthouse tower. From the immediate vicinity of Bolivar Point practically all families sought refuge in the tower when the water

began to rise Monday afternoon, August 16 and from that time until late Tuesday afternoon they were forced to remain in their cramped quarters, although they were glad enough of the opportunity to so remain, in as much as during the night every moment had held the prospect of the great tube being hurled into the towering waves by the terrific wind.

H. C. Claiborne, keeper of Bolivar Light, who spent the night of the 1900 storm in the tower, declares that unquestionably the recent Texas coast storm was much more severe than its predecessor. The water, he says, was considerably higher and the wind more prolonged to almost four times the length of the 1900 hurricane. In the storm of that year none of the lighthouse station houses were wrecked, whereas in the recent storm all structures save the residence of the keeper were swept away and even that building was damaged.

J. P. Brooks, first assistant keeper, who was on watch during the early part of the night of the recent storm, declared that the big tower shook and swayed in the wind like a giant reed, while every moment he

The Harry Claiborne *is ready to slide into the water. Marinette Marine Corporation photo.*

Ms. Nancy E. McFadden, General Counsel, US Department of Transportation, christens the ship with the traditional bottle of champagne. Marinette Marine Corporation photo.

The Harry Claiborne *hits the water with a spectacular splash. Marinette Marine Corporation photo.*

expected to feel the structure crumbling beneath his feet or to have the heavy glass windows of the lamp crushed in upon him.

At 9:15 o'clock Monday night the mechanism which rotates the lantern was put out of commission by the furious swaying of the tower and from that time until 10 o'clock Mr. Brooks turned the big lamp by hand, clinging to the crank and working away as best he could while the wind rose higher and higher and the tower ever swayed wider and wider in its teeth.

At 10 o'clock the vibration was so great that it became impossible to keep the lamp rotating at all. Mr. Brooks accordingly trimmed the mantles of the lantern and left it burning. Descending to the foot of the tower he found another hazardous task awaiting him. The water had risen until it was neck deep over the tower floor and the big iron door

The Harry Claiborne joins four of her sisterships waiting for finishing touches before delivery to the Coast Guard. Marinette Marine Corporation photo.

> which gives entrance at the base had been dashed open by the wind. It became necessary to get this door closed to protect the tower from the wash of the current and Mr. Brooks, armed with a rope, essayed to make fast the barrier. He was badly battered and bruised by the wind and waves before the task was accomplished, but it was done at last.
>
> Christopher Morris, the second assistant keeper, during the night, slipped and fell on the narrow circular stairway, badly spraining an ankle, which rendered him unable to assist in any work for the remainder of the storm.
>
> The light was kept burning throughout the night of the storm, but the next night and the next - Wednesday and Thursday - it did not burn, the first time since it was built, nearly a half century ago, that it failed to shine for such an extended period. The reason for the eclipse was a lack of oil. The big tanks which contain the oil supply of the station were broken up and swept away by the wind and water and the lantern was left without fuel. It was two days before it was possible to procure a supply by boat from Galveston and during those two nights, therefore, the familiar beacon was not to be seen.[4]

Up and down the Gulf Coast other lights were also damaged. At Sabine Pass, Louisiana, the wharf and all outbuildings were swept away as well as the East Jetty Light, Inner Range Lights, and Channel Light. The Fort San Jacinto Lighthouse Depot in Texas was completely washed away, including all of the buoys and supplies. It seems every lighthouse suffered some form of damage.

What nature couldn't destroy, sometimes man can. Bolivar Light was one of the very few lighthouses ever to come under artillery fire. The U.S. Army's Coast Artillery at Ft. San Jacinto was expending old ammunition, not realizing it still had enough punch to reach the lighthouse. The result was a three-inch hole in the tower just above the door. Claiborne was not a happy lightkeeper! He could understand hurricanes trying to knock down his tower–but the Army?

Claiborne retired in 1918 and was replaced by his assistant, J. B. Brooks. Before the year was out Claiborne was dead at age 59. He had been a dedicated lightkeeper for 31 years but it was his compassion for others, as evidenced by the great hurricanes of 1900 and 1915, that truly distinguished his life. Bolivar Light burned a little dimmer the night he died.[5]

Footnotes

1. Clarence Ousley. *Galveston in Nineteen Hundred,* (Atlanta: William C. Chase, 1900), p. 23.

2. Ousley, *Galveston,* p. 23.

3. Ousley, *Galveston,* p. 27.

4. *Lighthouse Service Bulletin*, October 1915, pp. 182-183.

5. *Annual Report of the Commissioner of Lighthouses to the Secretary of Commerce* (Washington, DC: Government Printing Office, 1916); "Bolivar Lighthouse," [http://www.crystalbeach.com/light.htm], February 12, 1999; *Galveston Daily News,* August 30, 1915; *Lighthouse Service Bulletin,* October 1915, pp. 181-182, November 1915, pp. 185-186; Herbert Molloy Mason, Jr., *Death From the Sea, Our Greatest Natural Disaster, the Galveston Hurricane of 1900* (New York: Dial Press, 1972), pp. 162-166; "Naming File," U.S. Coast Guard Historian's Office, Washington DC; Clarence Ousley, *Galveston in Nineteen Hundred,* (Atlanta: William C. Chase, 1900), pp. 40-51.

The Cutters

THE KEEPER CLASS

VESSEL	HOME PORT	DELIVERY DATE
Ida Lewis (WLM-551)	Newport, RI	November 1, 1996
Katherine Walker (WLM-552)	Bayonne, NJ	June 27, 1997
Abbie Burgess (WLM-553)	Rockland, ME	September 19, 1997
Marcus Hanna (WLM-554)	Portland, ME	November 26, 1997
James Rankin (WLM-555)	Baltimore, MD	August 26, 1998
Joshua Appleby (WLM-556)	St. Petersburg, FL	November 20, 1998
Frank Drew (WLM-557	Portsmouth, VA	June 17, 1999
Anthony Petit (WLM-558)	Ketchikan, AK	July 1, 1999
Barbara Mabrity (WLM-559)	Mobile, AL	July 29, 1999
William Tate (WLM-560)	Philadelphia, PA	September 16, 1999
Henry Clairborne (WLM-561)	Galveston, TX	November 18, 1999
Maria Bray (WLM-562)	Charleston, SC	May 18, 2000
Henry Blake (WLM-563)	Seattle, WA	June 22, 2000
George Cobb (WLM-564)	San Pedro, CA	September 28, 2000

KEEPER CLASS COASTAL BUOY TENDER

MISSIONS

Aids to Navigation
Marine Environmental Protection
Search and Rescue
Domestic Ice Breaking

PRINCIPAL CHARACTERISTICS

Length . . . . 175 feet
Beam . . . . 36 feet
Draft (Full Load). . . . . 8 Feet, 5 Inches
Displacement (Full Load). . . . . 840 Long Tons
Buoy Deck Area . . . . . . 1,335 Square Feet
Officers 1
Enlisted 17

EQUIPMENT

Main Engines . . 2 CAT 3508, 999 BHP @ 1600 RPM
Propulsion . . 2 Ulstein 1350 360° Steerable Z-Drives
Thruster . . . . 500 HP/DC Fixed Pitch
Power Generators . . . . 3 CAT 3406 285 KW each
Crane . . . . . . 10 Ton Hydraulic, 42 Foot Boom

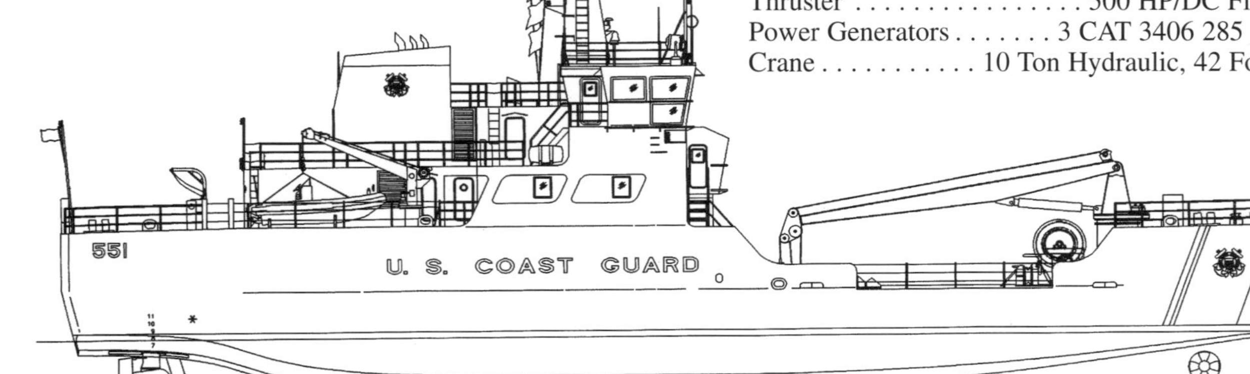

XVI
Marinette Marine Corporation

Telling the story of the Keeper-Class cutters and their namesakes requires understanding the unique company that built them–Marinette Marine Corporation of Marinette, Wisconsin. Located deep in the Great Lakes, this very special company, and the hardworking men and women that are its greatest resource, has proven itself to be a world leader in commercial, research and military applications. It is important to realize that while Marinette Marine is located in Marinette on the Wisconsin side of the Menominee River, on the opposite side is the city of Menominee, Michigan. By drawing its workers from both cities, the company enjoys an immense advantage in human resources.

Marinette Marine has built more than 1,200 vessels–out of aluminum, steel and wood, ranging up to 400 feet in length. The 20-acre shipyard runs along 1,200 feet of the Menominee River. The company is especially proud of its carefully structured organization, including a very finely tuned system for planning, organizing and scheduling every phase of an operation. From design and engineering to quality control and inspection, Marinette Marine excels at it all.

The company was founded on April 14, 1942, by Marinette physician Clarence Boren and Milwaukee businessman Max Hellermann to help meet the country's increasing needs for naval construction during World War II. Marinette, might be far from the battlefront, but it could contribute importantly to the war effort. Hellermann had previously studied marine engineering, so he had an understanding of the job he was starting. The pair

The first wooden barge is laid out for construction. Marinette Marine Corporation photo.

purchased a site on the Menominee River to build their shipyard and the company was off and running.

Within two months, the new company submitted a proposal to the U. S. Maritime Commission for the building of several cargo barges. On June 17, 1942, it received a contract for five 192-foot non-powered wood barges. Known as White Pine-Class barges, they were constructed of green lumber, most of which came from the nearby Wisconsin and Michigan forests. The first two barges were launched to the thundering cheers of 15,000 spectators on May 23, 1943, three months to the day, that the keel of the first barge was laid. Prior to the barge contract being completed, the Maritime Commission gave the company another for six wooden 65-foot, self-propelled tugs intended to be used in combination with the barges. Before the war was over, the company also built prefabricated steel bulkheads for famous Victory-class cargo ships and parts for metallic pontoon assault bridges. Marinette Marine achieved an enviable reputation for its efficiency. From 1943 until the end of war, the company flew the Navy "E" for Excellence at the flagpole, as well as the Minuteman flag, both honoring the company as a firm that was able to get the job done.

As the war was winding down, company management knew they would have to find new products to build for a vastly different postwar market.

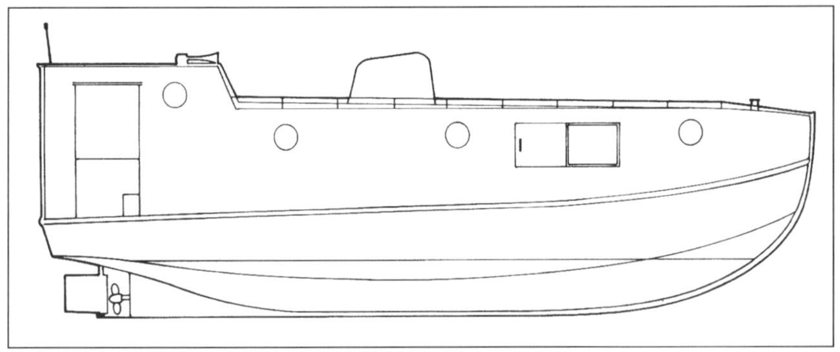

A sketch of the 36-foot fish tugs. Marinette Marine Corporation Collection.

Commercial fishing was still a major economic force on the Great Lakes and fishermen needed good boats. It was a market they could prosper in. Eventually the company built thirty-one, 36-foot diesel-powered steel fish tugs and a number of 42-footers. Marinette Marine also built freezers for farm and home use, oil well drilling equipment, wheelbarrows, truck trailers and mining equipment. Whatever the private market needed, the company could produce.

But someone in the Federal Government remembered the high quality work the little shipyard far away in the backwaters of Wisconsin did during the war, because in 1952, the U.S. Army Corps of Engineers awarded a contract for four river tow boats. It wasn't much, but it helped the company stay alive and it kept them visible in the government's eyes.

A view of the shipyard in 1946. Marinette Marine Corporation photo.

Changes were coming at the company. In 1954, Harold Derusha, who started with the company as a mechanic in 1942, and had worked his way up to yard superintendent, was able to purchase a majority interest in the yard. Derusha wisely focused the company on getting more involved in the government markets. He also centered the company's work on water craft and military floating bridge components, focussing on what it did best. Again, the Federal Government remembered Marinette Marine, and in 1955 it received a contract for one hundred and forty-eight, 56-foot, mechanized landing craft, known as LCM (Landing Craft, Mechanized). Private industry also recognized the quality of the company's work. The Arnold Transit Line, one of two ferry operators at Michigan's world-famous Mackinac Island, ordered the 65-foot steel ferry, *Mohawk*. Using the contracts as a basis, the company became expert at steel fabrication and production line construction. Increasingly it grew in its ability to use new technologies. The highly skilled and stable work force gave the company an advantage that other shipyards often lacked. It was an advantage the company would use many times in the years ahead. By the time the 1950s drew to a close, Marinette Marine had built 121 small craft for the Army Corps of Engineers and 220 for the Navy. Production was so efficient that at one point a 56-foot LCM was produced every two days and a 36-foot LCP (Landing Craft, Personnel) *every 14 minutes!*

During the 1960s through the1980s, the company continued to build a variety of vessels for the government and civilian market. Each one allowed the company to gain experience, to grow in technological, managerial and design prowess. In their own way, each was also a stepping stone to the next project–critical preparation in the art of working in wood, steel and

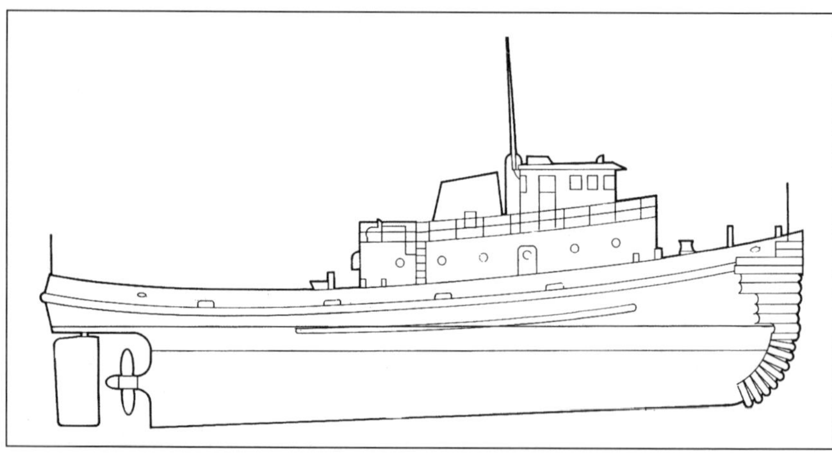

A sketch of a YTB tug. Marinette Marine Corporation photo.

aluminum. Although the company built many types of vessels during this period, including gunboats, torpedo retrievers, pilot boats, landing craft and tugs, some projects stand out as crucial to its development.

In 1962, the Navy awarded a contract for two 209-foot oceanographic research ships. Not only were the ships large, but also the most sophisticated the yard ever built. Great innovation was needed to solve problems concerning the propulsion system, general space arrangement and noise reduction. Finished in the summer of 1965, the *Thomas G. Thompson* was delivered to the University of Washington and the *Thomas Washington*, to the Scripps Institute in LaJolla, California.

As the role of the U.S. in Southeast Asia increased in the 1960s, Marinette Marine received its largest contract to date. In 1964, eight YTB harbor tugs were ordered by the Navy. Each was 109 feet overall, with a beam of 29 feet. These new tugs could develop 2,000 horsepower, twice the power of previous tugs. Based on the success of the first eight, Marinette Marine received an order for eight more in 1965, with additional orders following through 1973, until a total of 50 had been built! The YTBs, all built on the shores of the Menominee River, performed duty all over the world

A strength of Marinette Marine has always been its use of cutting edge technology. Five of the YTBs ordered in 1967 were the last vessels the company ever built using the old mold loft to develop the lines. From then on, a state-of-the-art optical steel burning machine cut the steel by following lines on paper. Computer-controlled lofting became the standard for such work at Marinette Marine. This new method was more accurate and efficient. Prior to this time, the lines of the hull were drawn out full size on wood or paper templates, which in turn were used to produce the actual pieces of the vessel. This method of "lofting" or "laying off" has been used for centuries.

The only constant is change and this was true for Marinette Marine. On March 1, 1975, Harold Derusha retired as President of Marinette Marine, and his son Roger Derusha was named President of the Corporation and Chairman of the Board. Harold continued to support the company as a member of the board and consultant.

As early as 1971, the yard was using numerically controlled burning of plates with acetylene. Continuing to improve technology, in 1975 a computer-guided plasma burner was added to the yard. To make the system work, the Engineering Department developed the details of the needed steel shape and translated the specifications into computer disks which in turn controlled the computer-burning equipment. The new system provided speed, accessibility and accuracy in the lofting of ships. It also greatly reduced the number of blueprints needed. It was said the blueprints for the World War II battleship

T-ATF Narragansett *hits the river! Marinette Marine Corporation photo.*

Iowa weighed 750 tons. Massive paperwork was a problem that would always haunt the company, especially as evidenced in government contracts and bids.

As the 1970s drew to a close, the company delivered its largest self-propelled vessel yet, the lead ship in a contract for T-ATF fleet tugs for the Navy Sea Systems Command. These ships were designed to replace the World War II-era ATF fleet tugs that had seen extensive duty. The tugs were 226 feet long, 42 feet in beam, and had a full displacement of 2,260 tons. Each was powered by two diesels developing a total of 7,200 horsepower with a pull of 120,000 tons. At 13 knots, cruising range was 10,000 miles. They had controllable-pitch propellers, and large aft decks allowing helicopter operations as well as space for salvage equipment. The tugs were designed above all for salvage work and towing battle-damaged or inoperable ships. Extremely capable vessels, they could also perform rescue operations, fire fighting, diving and oil-spill recovery. A total of seven of the tugs were built. The Navy named them *Powhatan*, *Narragansett*, *Catawba*, *Navajo*, *Mohawk*, *Sioux* and *Apache*. The *Apache* distinguished herself in September 1982, by towing the battleship *Iowa* from the Philadelphia Naval Shipyard to Westwego, Louisiana, for modernization, preparatory to returning to active service.

Working at Marinette Marine had also become a family affair. The men and women of the company were in many cases the sons and daughters (and

The research vessel Shell America. *Marinette Marine Corporation photo.*

in some cases the grandchildren) of the original crews who started building the pine barges in 1942!

In 1982, the company contracted for the 300-foot, 5,340 ton *Shell America*. The seismic research vessel, one of the most advanced in the world, was built to cruise the oceans searching for new deposits of oil and natural

The 224-foot Mine Counter Measure ship USS Patriot. *Marinette Marine Corporation photo.*

gas. The ship accommodates a crew of 53 in 28 staterooms, each with a private bath and climate controls.

During the early 1980s, the yard received a Navy contract to assist in the evaluation of a proposed new mine-sweeping vessel. Known as the Avenger-Class Mine Countermeasure (MCM), these 224-foot wooden hull vessels would be the first mine-sweepers built since the Korean War. Before the evaluation was completed, Marinette Marine was selected as one of two shipyards to build the new MCM class. Forty years after building wooden barges the company was again building with wood! Most sea mines react to the magnetic signature of a ship's hull. Building the mine hunters out of non-metallic materials greatly reduces this signature and improves vessel survivability. These ships were designed as mine hunter-killers, capable of finding, classifying and destroying moored and bottom mines. They use sonar and video systems, and remote controlled cable cutters and mine-detonating devices. Their wood hulls are sheathed in fiberglass. Four turbo-charged diesels provided a speed of 13.5 knots.

In 1993, Daniel Gulling, an executive with the nearby Cruiser's Incorporated in Oconto, Wisconsin, assembled a group of investors and purchased the company. Roger Derusha in turn, became Chairman of the Board of the new Marinette Marine Corporation.

The company was also selected to participate in the Coast Guard's visionary Deepwater Project. Deepwater is a project consisting of ships, aircraft, communications and sensors designed to work together to increase the Coast Guard's operational effectiveness. It is not a one-for-one replacement of ships and aircraft with newer versions. Instead, it is a complete system, a new way of doing business. Three separate contractor teams were selected, representing a wide degree of experience and technology applications. Marinette Marine was paired with several companies, including the Bath Iron Works, Gibbs and Co. and Sikorsky Helicopter. The teams were charged with starting the initial conceptual development of the Deepwater Project. The system would include air and surface equipment, command, control, communications, computers, intelligence, sensors and reconnaissance, and the supporting logistical structure. Central to the project is the construction of a class of ships to replace the Coast Guard's high-endurance and medium-endurance cutters. The project is considered to be critical to the operational future of the Coast Guard.

Marinette Marine Corporation executed a comprehensive systems engineering approach to its design and its plan to build the U.S. Coast Guard's new class of seagoing and coastal buoy tenders. This approach started with a survey of existing U.S. and foreign buoy tenders which are

Marinette Marine Corporation shipyard as it appeared on May 11, 1997. Marinette Marine Corporation photo.

performing similar duties. Information obtained through literature surveys, and visits to the Dutch buoy tender *Rotterdam* and the Swedish buoy tender *Baltica,* was compared to the Coast Guard's operational requirements of each vessel. The designs developed improved on these existing ships in innovation and cost effective ways to meet the U.S. Coast Guard's demanding requirements.

Shipbuilding, especially for the Federal Government, has become far more complicated than just building the best vessel possible for the lowest cost. For example, from inception by the Coast Guard to the launch of the first of Juniper-class cutter, it took *ten years!* The paper work is also astounding! Marinette Marine's bid proposal to build the new tenders took 18 months to assemble, and weighed 1,200 pounds! Six copies had to be made

From the first plate of steel to launching, typically takes eight months. Construction is highly modular and extremely efficient. As sections are finished, they are mated together and additional components added until she is ready for launching. Marinette Marine Corporation photos.

and sent to Washington, finally being submitted in October 1992. Had the Coast Guard not accepted the bid, all was wasted time, effort and money.

The company's extensive experience with government red tape, worked to its advantage, however. The bid was awarded in two stages. The best three bids of the nine received went to the second stage for closer review and evaluation. The result was that in January of 1993, Marinette Marine was awarded the contract for the lead ship of the Juniper Class, the 225-foot tender. Five months later the company received the contract for the lead ship of the Keeper-Class 175-foot tenders. In time, the company earned the contracts for all 14 of the Keeper Class as well as the entire Juniper Class.

There is more to building a cutter than simply launching it and watching it sail away. The company also has to provide warranty, manuals, repair parts, support and testing, and crew training. All of these critical items must be factored into a bid.

The reasons the company received the contract are many. Marinette Marine has perfected highly efficient, modular, subassembly and assembly methods. A continual investment in state-of-the-art manufacturing technologies, and the development of integrated engineering methods and project management systems, provided the capability to build vessels in the most efficient manner possible. A quality-minded corporate culture and strong work ethic are company characteristics. As a result of the company's past performance, the U.S. Navy has designated Marinette Marine as a "Premier Supplier," a rare honor. President Dan Gulling summed it up by saying, "We had two very creative designs for the Coast Guard ships, and it's the design efficiency that got us the business. The Coast Guard is very happy with our quality. It's a talented group of people here, and they're very dedicated, and they take pride in what they do."

XVII
The United States Coast Guard

The New Tenders

In many ways the new 175-foot Keeper-Class (coastal) tender and 225-foot Juniper-Class (seagoing) tender are strikingly similar. The comment has been made that the 225-footer is really just a 175-footer on steroids! To the layman's eye they can be easily confused.

Design–Both vessels are configured with a large working deck forward of the deckhouse, providing excellent visibility for conducting buoy-handling operations. This configuration was selected because it provides for improved crew familiarity, with operator orientation remaining forward at all times. It also has the added benefits of improving crew comfort by locating accommodations aft where ship motions are generally less severe, and by improving survivability in case of damage by incorporating a forecastle and a raised poop deck aft. Below decks, the machinery spaces, engineer's control center, and shops are centrally located with convenient access to all storerooms and maintenance activities. Fore and aft access is provided throughout the vessel via quick-acting watertight doors.

The control booth for conducting buoy-handling operations is located conveniently to and with direct access to the buoy deck. Visibility from the control booth has been enhanced by providing full-length windows to port and starboard of the buoy deck control console. The pilothouse of each vessel has also been arranged to provide improved access to ship control functions and excellent visibility forward and aft.

A critical point in both designs was minimizing crew size by increasing automation. The most expensive item in any budget is always personnel. Anything that can decrease the number of men and women to crew the vessel is important. Where a 180-footer might have a crew of 49, a new Keeper Class is designed for 18 personnel and the Juniper Class for 40.

Engines–Perhaps the most notable characteristic of the two tenders is the incorporation of the associated propulsion system in each design. The 225-foot vessel has been provided with a single shaft plus bow and stern thruster arrangement, while the 175-foot tender has twin Z-drive propulsion thrusters in lieu of conventional propellers and rudders. The selection of these propulsion systems was the result of extensive requirements analysis and trade-off studies performed at the beginning the each design process. The resulting propulsion systems were selected because they meet or exceed the specific requirements of each class vessel. They also offer maximum maneuverability and operational flexibility at minimum cost. Both ships can turn within their own length.

Deck Operations–Port and starboard buoy ports located on the forward end of the buoy deck and buoy storage facilities aft (rear) on the buoy deck adjacent to the deckhouse. A chain-handling winch is located on centerline at the forward end of buoy deck. This chain-handling winch allows the operator to haul in a variety of chain sizes linked in series without having to halt operations. This capability minimizes the number of personnel involved in the operation and maximizes its safety aspects. The concept of a continuous-chain winch was one that was completely new to the U.S. ship- and buoy-handling operations. The winch was designed and developed by Marinette Marine's engineering staff.

In addition, there is a manual and power-assisted four-point buoy-tie-down system. This MMC-originated design allows proper and safe handling of the buoys with a minimum of personnel.

Dynamic Positioning System–The Juniper and Keeper tenders are provided with a dynamic positioning system that allows the ships to approach, maneuver, and automatically maintain position within a circle of 10 meters in radius over a fixed point on the earth. The dynamic positioning system utilizes the Global Positioning System (GPS) to maintain the ship's position. The Juniper-Class vessels can hold position in open water with winds up to 30 knots and seas with wave heights of eight feet. In restricted waters of 18 foot depth or greater, it is able to perform satisfactorily in currents up to three knots, with the axis of the current within six degrees of the longitudinal centerline of the ship. If differential GPS is available, accuracy to maintain the ship in a circle of a two-meter radius is possible.

Keeper Class performance is similar, in conditions of somewhat lesser wind and sea conditions.

Digital Data Communications System–The tenders are provided with a digital data communications system that accommodates the data necessary for the proper operation, maintenance, and administration of the ship. The digital data communication system includes a Local Area Network (LAN) and the Automatic Data Processing (ADP) equipment necessary to support the LAN.

The LAN is a fiberoptic network that is capable of collecting, storing, and distributing the various data elements utilized in the day-to-day functions of the ship. The LAN, too, is a Survivable, Adaptable Fiberoptic-Embedded Network, known as SAFENET, which includes redundant fiberoptic cable rings to insure adequate fault tolerance and survivability. A sampling of this data includes tactical information, navigation information, dynamic positioning system data, interior communications data, and machinery operational and maintenance data–and the various alarms located throughout. the ships. The ADP equipment is capable to support administrative communications such as electronic mail and file transfers, as well as logistics communication data (such as financial and supply data).

Integrated Bridge System–Both tenders have an "Integrated" bridge that is capable of utilizing inputs from the ships production control system, dynamic positioning system and other appropriate data that has been input into the SAFENET system. This system provides instantaneous data to the Commanding Officer and minimizes the number of personnel necessary to safely conn the ship.

Electronic Chart Display Information System (ECDIS)–Both classes are equipped with the state-of-the-art ECDIS. This system processes information from all of the ship's navigational sensors such as radar, LORAN, DGPS, gyro compass, and speed log to display the ship's real time position, heading, and speed on an electronic chart.

Marine Environmental Protection–The tenders have been designed and equipped to provide a complete spilled oil recovery system for removing petroleum spills from navigable waters and the open ocean. The system includes port and starboard floating sweep arms which recover the spilled oil (and water) and pump it via deck hose connections to separation tanks in the vessel. The oil is then separated from the water by gravity, water is pumped overboard, and the oil is pumped to stem and alongside deck connections to a towed oil storage Dracone[1] or a vessel of opportunity.[2] This is also referred to as a VOSS, or Vessel of Opportunity Skimming System. It is only used on the Keeper Class. The vessel is also provisioned with an oil storage Dracone

This photo shows four of the Keeper-Class tenders, William Tate, Barbara Mabrity, Petit, Frank Drew *and* William Claiborne *at Marinette Marine. Marinette Marine Corporation photo.*

and 200 meters of oil containment boom. The spilled oil recovery systems (SORS–Juniper Class only) pumps are located in a dedicated compartment which contains only SORS equipment, thus simplifying operations.

Search-and-Rescue (SAR)–The tenders contain surface search and navigational radar, communication equipment, medical equipment, and other navigational aids necessary to conduct proper search and rescue operations. The ships are also equipped with high-speed small boats to assist in this operation.

There also are some very significant differences between the two designs that are rooted deeply in the intended missions for the vessels.

Keeper Class

Perhaps the most notable characteristic of the Keeper Class is the incorporation of twin Z-drive propulsion thrusters in lieu of conventional propellers and rudders. The selection of this propulsion system was the result

The Z-drive is clearly visible. Author's photo.

The bridge of a Keeper-Class tender is highly functional. Marinette Marine Corporation photo.

of extensive requirements analysis and trade-off study performed at the beginning of the design process. The selection of the Z-drive methodology provides maximum maneuverability at minimum costs. The Z-drive model selected for the Keeper-Class tender provides the Coast Guard the ability to replace the Z-drive underwater unit without the need to drydock the ship. This permits convenient periodic maintenance and fast turn around if replacement of a unit is necessary.

Size–The tenders are 174 feet, 8 inches in length with a 36-foot beam, and displace 916 long tons, draw 8 feet, 4 inches, and provide 1,335 square feet of buoy deck. It has a fixed-length boom hydraulic crane located at the forward end of the buoy deck.

Deck Crane–

- 10-ton capacity main hoist.
- 3.75-ton capacity secondary or whip hoist.
- 42-foot-long, boom.
- Crane control cab integrated into deckhouse front below pilothouse.

Propulsion–Includes two main diesel engines, 999 BHP per unit, driving two propellers through right angle, azimuthing propulsion thrusters (Z-drives):

- Two propellers, Each 5 feet, 5 inches in diameter, fixed-pitch propellers.
- Bow thruster, 400 HP, fixed-pitch propeller tunnel drive, electrically powered.

The bow thruster provides critical maneuverability. Marinette Marine Corporation photo.

The mechanical spaces reflect state of the art equipment. Marinette Marine Corporation photos.

With both Z-drives hard over and the bow thruster activated, the Frank Drew *spins on it's own axis, demonstrating great maneuverability. Marinette Marine Corporation photo.*

The Anthony Petit *goes full astern during testing. Marinette Marine Corporation photo.*

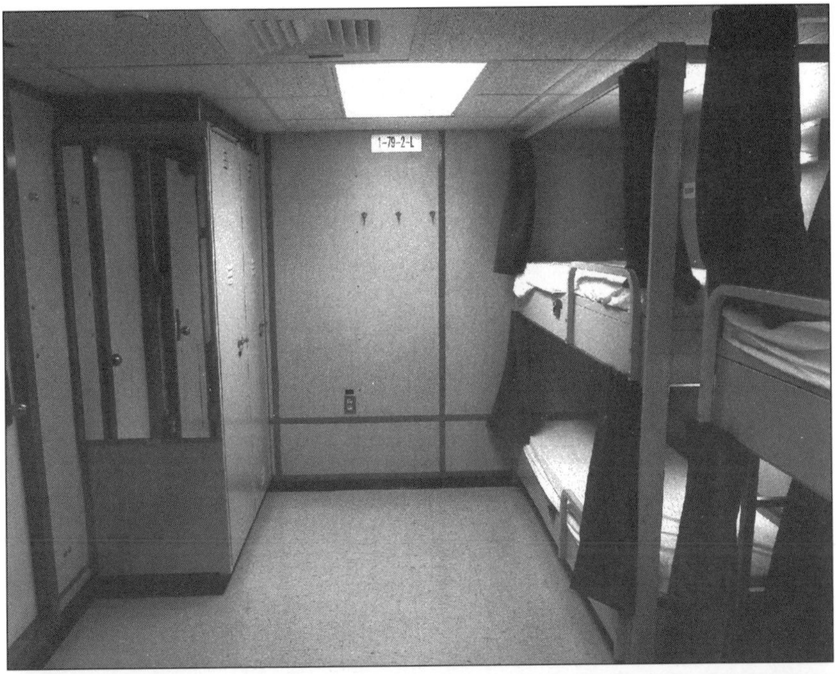

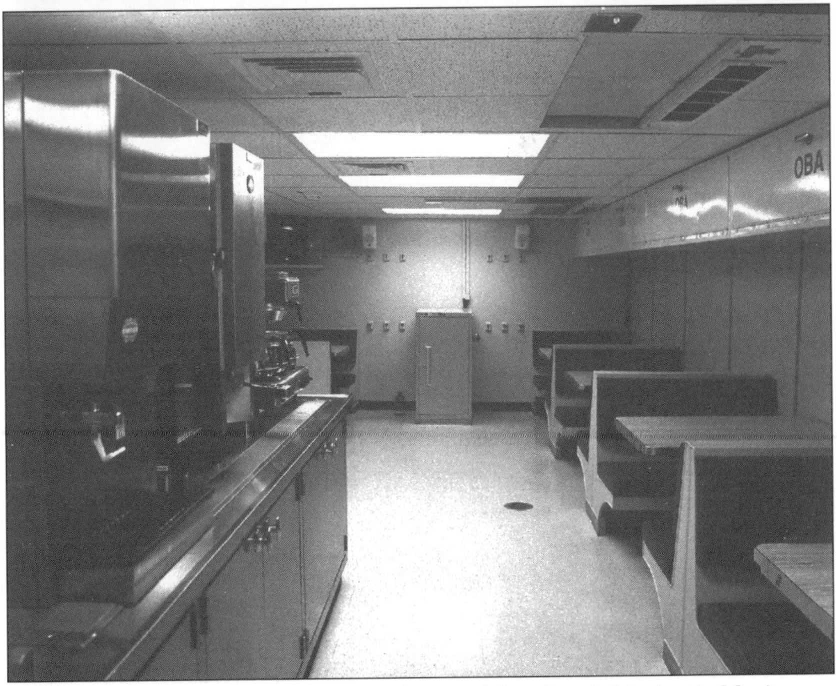

Berthing and galley spaces are spacious and functional. Marinette Marine Corporation photo.

• Electrical system that includes three ship-service-class generators, providing 60 hertz/250 kw per unit, and one emergency diesel generator with 60 Hertz/250 kw.

With the Z-drives and bow thruster, a Keeper-Class ship can virtually spin on its turning axis. The class has incredible maneuverability, a critical item for a buoy tender.

Steering–Steering is via a single rudder, driven by an electro-hydraulic steering system, and bilge keels to improve roll response and stabilization.

Habitability–The coastal buoy tender accommodates a crew of 18 personnel. The vessel is designed to provide berthing for both male and female personnel.

Speed and Range–The tenders are capable of maintaining a speed of 12 knots at full load displacement in calm water. The cutter has a range of 2,000 nautical miles at a speed of 10 knots in a full load condition.

Ice Operations–The tenders are capable of breaking nine inches of fresh water ice at three knots continuous speed, and a minimum of 18 inches of fresh water ice by ramming. The Juniper class, being larger, has increased capability.

Juniper, *the lead ship in the Juniper-Class tenders, underway in river ice. Marinette Marine Corporation photo.*

Juniper Class

Size–The Juniper-Class tender is 225 feet in length, has a 46-foot beam, displaces approximately 2000 long tons, draws 13 feet in salt water and provides 2,875 square feet of buoy deck working space

Deck Crane–The hydraulic operated boom crane is capable of lifting 20 tons from the main hoist and five tons from the secondary or whip hoist. The crane's main hoist has a maximum reach of 60 feet and is capable of being retracted to 30 feet.

Propulsion–The Juniper Class is propelled by two Caterpillar Diesel engines, each capable of 3,100 shaft horsepower (SHP). They provide thrust (through a reduction gear) to a single shaft equipped with a ten-foot-diameter, four-blade controllable and reversible pitch propeller. Juniper is capable of maintaining a speed of 15 knots at full load displacement, and an endurance (at 12 knots) of no less than 21 days without replenishment.

Maneuvering–Maneuvering the vessel in restricted waters is enhanced by the addition of bow and stern thrusters. The 460-SHP bow and 555-SHP stem thrusters are fixed-pitch tunnel-type units. They are powered by

The Juniper's *bridge is larger than the Keeper-Class. Marinette Marine Corporation photo.*

Whether outside or inside, Marinette Marine Corporation launch ceremonies are always a very popular affair. Author's photos.

The end of the line. A Coast Guard crew prepares to accept the tender. Marinette Marine Corporation photo.

appropriately sized electric motors which are electrically driven by a single generator. The generator's prime mover is provided through the use of a power takeoff unit attached to the ship's reduction gear. Steering is accomplished through an electro-hydraulic steering system which drives a single rudder located just aft of the propeller.

Seakeeping and Survivability–The Juniper-Class ships provide a suitable working platform to replace buoy hardware or repair buoys (including signal and mooring equipment) when the ship is operating in winds up to 30 knots, and in seas with wave heights of eight feet. The natural roll period of the ship will be no less than eight seconds under any loading conditions. Juniper-Class ships meet the damage stability requirements with respect to two compartment flooding.

Habitability–The Juniper-Class ships accommodate a minimum of six officers, four chief petty officers, and 30 enlisted personnel. Separate accommodations are provided for the commanding officer and the executive

Keeper Class Coastal Buoy Tender

Missions

Aids to Navigation
Marine Environmental Protection
Search and Rescue
Domestic Ice Breaking

Principal Characteristics

Length	*175 feet*
Beam	*36 feet*
Draft (Full Load)	*8 Feet, 5 Inches*
Displacement (Full Load)	*840 Long Tons*
Buoy Deck Area	*1,335 Square Feet*
Officers	*1*
Enlisted	*17*

Equipment

Main Engines	*2 CAT 3508, 999 BHP @ 1600 RPM*
Propulsion	*2 Ulstein 1350 360° Steerable Z-Drives*
Thruster	*500 HP/DC Fixed Pitch*
Power Generators	*3 CAT 3406 285 KW each*
Crane	*10 Ton Hydraulic, 42 Foot Boom*

officer. Personnel accommodations provide for a reasonable level of crew alertness through the proper provision of noise abatement, vibration abatement, and other habitable provisions that reduce crew fatigue. Crew quarters are located aft of the buoy deck where ship motions are generally less severe.

Ice Operating Capabilities–The Juniper-Class ships are capable of three knots of continuous speed while operating in up to 14 inches of freshwater ice, and can break a minimum of 36 inches of packed, refrozen freshwater ice by ramming.

Defense and Security–Space and weight allowance are provided to install one MK438, Mod 0 25mm cannon and four 50-caliber machine guns. Magazines and an armory suitable to accommodate ammunition storage and small arms, (as well as the 50-caliber machine guns) have been designed into the hull. An area to accomplish the maintenance of the weapons is also provided.

The Mission

The primary mission of the new Keeper-Class tenders is to maintain what the Coast Guard calls "Aids to Navigation" or ATON. Specifically, the tenders will focus on the short-range aids as opposed to the longer range ones such as charts, satellite systems like GPS or radio systems like LORAN. Short-range aids are used by vessel navigators to determine their position, follow a safe course and avoid dangers and obstructions. These aids are external to the vessel and are located along coasts and navigable waters. They include buoys, day beacons, lights, radar beacons and sound signals.

ATON have been used in the United States since the 18th century. The first lighthouse was built in Boston harbor in 1716. Small wooden buoys called spar buoys were first used in the Delaware River near Philadelphia in 1767. Such aids were officially legislated through the Ninth Act of the First Session of Congress in 1789, which directed the construction and maintenance of lighthouses under the Lighthouse Service. Responsibility for the day-to-day operation of the various aids was given to the Treasury Department. A total of 12 lighthouses and seven buoys were transferred from state to federal control. In 1792, floating beacons were introduced for the first time in Chesapeake Bay.

Under an 1838 Act of Congress, lighthouse districts were formed. The Atlantic Coast was divided into six districts and the Great Lakes into two. A naval officer was appointed to each district and assigned the job of inspecting all aids to navigation, report on their condition and make recommendations. Lighthouse tenders were first introduced in 1840. Their job was to assume all of the lighthouse tending and buoy maintenance previously done by chartered or contract vessels.

In 1852 the Lighthouse Board was created to better manage the growing system of aids. Thc Board was transferred to the Department of Commerce in 1903, and in 1910 it was abolished and a new Bureau of Lighthouses established. The Bureau was consolidated with the Coast Guard in 1939, under the Treasury Department.

The early 20th century saw the introduction of many new aids to navigation. Acetylene gas buoys, reinforced concrete lighthouses, diaphones for producing fog signals, semaphore signals, radio beacons, metal cone buoys, radio fog signals, gong buoys, range lanterns, aluminum buoys, battery-powered electric solenoid fog bell strikers, and radio beacon buoys. By 1939,

WLB 393 Firebush *is an example of a seagoing buoy tender. USCG photo.*

Katmai Bay *is an example of a WTGB. Author's photo.*

when the Bureau of Lighthouses merged with the Coast Guard, there were 39,000 aids being maintained.

The Coast Guard was transferred to the Department of Transportation in 1967. As the century continued, technology improvements resulted in the introduction of new types of aids: battery- and solar-powered buoys and beacons, radar beacons, sound signals, sector lights and ranges. From 1972 to 1993, the number of aids increased from 45,000 to 50,000. The job just keeps getting bigger!

The Coast Guard uses several types of vessel to service ATON.

- WLB–A large, stable, heavy-lift seagoing buoy tender servicing the largest buoys located in the roughest water farthest from shore.
- WLM–A lighter coastal buoy tender servicing medium-sized buoys in coastal waters such as bays, harbors and coastal channels.
- WTGB/Barge–An icebreaking tug pushing a crane-equipped barge servicing heavy buoys in semi-exposed locations. This combination is only used on the Great Lakes.
- WLI–An inland buoy tender operating in rivers and less exposed inland waterways, servicing small to medium buoys.
- WLIC–An inland construction tender that builds, or rebuilds if destroyed, fixed aids to navigation, including day beacons and minor lights.
- WLR–A river buoy tender consisting of a towboat with an attached barge carrying ATON equipment and a crane.

Shore-based Aids to Navigation Teams, (ANTs) are units that use a variety of small boats to service smaller ATON in protected waterways, and provide emergency support for aids normally serviced by vessel units.

The Coast Guard is constantly reviewing how its vessels are used in ATON support, as well as the effectiveness and efficiency of the various ATONs. How often should the aids be serviced or checked? What vessels are best suited for the various jobs? When are new vessels needed and what design would be best?

Old Tenders

There are an estimated 98,000 ATON in U.S. waters. Roughly 48,000 are privately owned and maintained. The rest are the responsibility of the Coast Guard.

To service the aids, the Coast Guard has a large fleet of various vessels as described earlier. Each type is designed for specific capabilities. For example, the big WLBs (seagoing tenders) would be appropriate for the large 24,000-pound, 9 by 38-foot whistle buoys in rough offshore waters. A WLR (river tender) would work best for a small 170-pound can buoy in shallow water.

The 180-foot buoy tender Sundew. *Brandon Stonehouse photo.*

All of the WLBs and most of the WLMs were built in the 1940s, and are well beyond their useful design lives, and will be replaced by the new Juniper- and Keeper-Class vessels. The WLBs are 180-foot vessels built by Marine Iron and Ship Building Company or Zenith Dredge Company, both in Duluth, Minnesota, during the 1941-44 period. The only exception was the *Ironwood*, built by the Coast Guard yard at Curtis Bay, Maryland. The original design of this class was worked up by the Lighthouse Service before it merged with the Coast Guard in 1939. The Lighthouse Service designed the vessels as pure tenders and for service in a specific area. Important characteristics for the Lighthouse Service work included twin screws for maneuverability, and shallow draft to allow approaching reefs and shoals close aboard. The Coast Guard, however, wanted multi-mission ships, able to perform a variety of jobs. The Coast Guard duly altered the original design to draw 13 feet, four feet more than the newest lighthouse tender, the 177-foot Juniper, built in 1939. They sacrificed twin screws for the increased immunity from ice damage of a single screw. The hull was also strengthened to provide some ice breaking ability.

A total of thirty-nine 180s were built in three sets. The first set included: *Cactus, Balsam, Cowslip, Woodbine, Gentian, Laureal, Clover, Evergreen, Sorrel, Citrus, Conifer, Madrona,* and *Tupelo*. The second consisted of: *Ironwood, Buttonwood, Planetree, Papaw, Sweetgum,* and *Mesquite*. The third set included: *Basswood, Bittersweet, Blackhaw, Blackthorn, Bramble, Firebush, Hornbeam, Iris, Mallow, Mariposa, Redbud, Sagebrush, Salvia, Sassafras, Sedge, Spar, Sundew, Sweetbrier, Acacia,* and *Woodrush*. Although all were of the same class, there were some minor differences in cost, shaft horsepower, and speed. Generally, speed was in the range of 13 knots on 1,200-shaft horsepower. Although crew size changed over the years, it was not uncommon to have a complement of three officers, two warrant officers and 42 men.

Many of the 180s saw World War II service in active theaters. The *Balsam* was credited with sinking a Japanese submarine with her depth charges. The *Mesquite* sailed with the famous Seventh Fleet and participated in the Philippines Campaign.

For their buoy tender work, these large, stable vessels are used to lift and service the heaviest buoys in the roughest seas farthest from shore. They also provide logistic support, including refueling isolated lights and stations, and National Ocean and Atmospheric Administration data buoys. To increase flexibility, they have two small boats aboard to allow work on two smaller buoys at the same time and service fixed aids. Of the 50,000 ATON, the WLBs service roughly 9 percent.

True to their Coast Guard design modifications, the 180s are multi-mission vessels. Their 21-day endurance and offshore ability allows them to perform many non-ATON missions. About 60 percent of their time is spent performing ATON servicing and 14 percent performing standard Coast Guard activities such as training. The rest of the time is spent on enforcement of laws and treaties (ELT), defense operations, search and rescue (SAR), marine science, marine environmental response (MER), and as needed, icebreaking. WLBs also participated in the cleanup efforts following the 1989, *Exxon Valdez* oil spill in Alaska. The 180s have fought ship fires, recovered downed aircraft, enforced fishing laws and treaties, towed disabled vessels, seized drug runners, as well as a host of other jobs. Whatever had to be done, the 180s did it.

The WLBs are also the only tenders with a wartime role outside the United States coastal area. Because of their great capabilities, they have been deployed to support mine-countermine operations, overseas ATON, and salvage.

The WLMs are smaller vessels than the WLBs, with shallower drafts and more limited endurance. They are intended to operate in coastal waters and under ideal conditions, can service all but the largest buoys. The WLMs also have small boats aboard to service fixed structures and smaller buoys. They have some limited icebreaking ability. Like the WLBs, they also perform ATON logistic support for isolated lights and their shallow draft allows them to work close inshore. About 3,050 or 6 percent of all ATON are serviced by WLMs. These vessels spent the greater part of their time, roughly 88 percent, working ATON. Standard Coast Guard activities take up 9 percent and other missions, the remainder.

There are two WLM classes. The 157-footers are somewhat less stable than other tenders and service the more sheltered bays and rivers of the Northeast and Mid-Atlantic Coast. There are five vessels in this class; *Red Wood, Red Beech, Red Birch, Red Cedar,* and *Red Oak*. All were built by the Coast Guard's Curtis Bay, Maryland yard between 1963-71. Twin screwed, they have a maximum speed of 13 knots. Crew size was five officers and 29 enlisted men. All are presently decommissioned

The 133-foot class is considered closer to the WLB in stability and services the more exposed areas in the Atlantic and Gulf Coasts. There were six vessels in this class. At present, only one is still in service.

The tender fleet is being augmented by WTGBs. These are icebreaking tugs that take on extra crew for the ATON mission. Nine of these tugs are in commission. Two of them are equipped with a 120-foot barge capable of lifting heavy buoys in semi-exposed locations, but due to the motion between tug and barge in rough water, operations are limited to calm conditions. Currently this combination is only used on the Great Lakes.

ATON Tomorrow

When the Coast Guard analyzed the future requirements of maintaining ATON, plus search and rescue, environmental response, and ELT (Enforcement of Laws and Treaties), it determined that they could best be met by a mix of 30 tenders. Sixteen would be the larger 225-foot Juniper-Class WLB, and 14 would be the smaller 175-foot Keeper-Class WLM. Of course, as mission requirements change, the best combination of these vessels and other smaller vessels also changes. The only constant in our world is change!

Over the past 40 years, ATON hardware technology improvements–such as changing from acetylene lamps needing quarterly service calls, to solar-powered electric lamps requiring annual services—has partially allowed a decline in the number of tenders from a high of 110 to 77 in 1993. New and improved technologies will doubtless decrease this number further.

Buoyant Beacons–The Coast Guard is testing buoyant beacons, which are essentially float chambers attached to a large sinker or anchor. Since the tension from the sinker tends to keep the structure upright, they resemble fixed aids rather than buoys. They are better able to withstand a collision, offer a more stable platform, and can mark channels with greater precision than conventional buoys. Such buoys are already in use in the Mediterranean Sea. The Coast Guard projects that they could require servicing only once every 10 years by the big Juniper- and Keeper-Class tenders.

Improved Lighting–The Coast Guard has recognized the need to improve ATON lighting. Powering them from shore is relatively cheap, but requires long underwater cables and outages can be anticipated from line faults or other accident. Diesel-generated power for large aids is attractive but needs frequent servicing. At remote sites, helicopter support is needed. High voltage solar arrays are powering some newer ATON but many panels are needed and the supporting structures and number of batteries can be extensive. Current lamp life is roughly one year for a six-lamp system. Longer lasting lamps and improved paint life could reduce service needs.

It is anticipated lighting improvements for minor lights and buoys will change little, since most are already solar-powered by inexpensive 12-volt systems. The exception is those lights powered by batteries. The batteries are considered an environmental hazard and need special handling for disposal. Improving battery life and efficiency is a constant goal.

Plastic Buoys–Buoys made from plastic may provide some advantages over the traditional steel in certain circumstances. They are easier to handle and need less maintenance than steel. Coast Guard experimentation with plastic and foam buoys in the 85- to 780-pound range shows they are very cost effective. However, they do have limitations. They are more easily damaged by ice and collision. Some countries have also tried fiberglass buoys up to 18,350 pounds, roughly the size of a 9-foot by 35-foot buoy, but the final results have not been evaluated. Other experimentation has looked at the use of nylon line to moor the sinker instead of conventional chain.

Navigational Needs–During the past half-century, the increased use of electronic navigation technologies such as radar, LORAN and GPS has decreased the need for traditional visible ATON. The use, especially among merchant vessels, of the new Electronic Chart Display and Information

System (ECDIS) using Differential GPS is expected to continue to increase. The ECDIS projects a chart on a computer screen and indicates the vessel position on it, along with data such as speed, course, etc. The Coast Guard continues to study the impact of new technologies on ATON.

The Deepwater Project

It is a little-known fact that (in 1999) the Deepwater Fleet of the Coast Guard, "deepwater" being defined as waters beyond 50 miles of shore, is the 39th oldest of 41 similar fleets in the world. Based on current worldwide building programs, it will soon fall to 40th. Coast Guard aircraft are also rapidly reaching the end of their projected life span.

To overhaul this outdated fleet of ships and aircraft, as well its communications, intelligence and control assets, and update them into the 21st century, the Coast Guard initiated the Deepwater Project. Deepwater is a comprehensive acquisition undertaking made up of vessels, airframes, communications, and intelligence gathering devices and methods designed to work together to increase the service's operational effectiveness. By no means is it a simple swapping of new ships and aircraft for old ones. Rather, it is a complete system fashioned to ease the workload of Coast Guard men and women so they can effectively carry out their missions. You cannot do more with less. The proper assets must be made available for the mission to succeed.

Current Coast Guard ships and aircraft can't always operate together. For example, HH-60 Jayhawk helicopters can't land on 210-foot or 378-foot cutters, but can land on 270-foot cutters. Similar integration problems exist with virtually all aspects of the service.

In most instances, the Coast Guard is operating with virtually 1950 to 1960-era technology. This is especially true in regard to law enforcement missions against drug smugglers. One area where the Coast Guard falls short is with its surveillance and communications equipment. Manned aircraft are often used to search for the criminals, but instead of radar, it's the eyeball that is mostly used. At night it is especially difficult. When a target is identified as "hot," a lack of voice-secure communications links requires the aircraft to return to base to make a report. Satellite surveillance could be the answer, if the Coast Guard vessels were equipped with integrated technology packages to use and disseminate the data.

The Deepwater Project came into focus in the early 1990s. The Coast Guard started to realize that their assets were approaching the end of their life cycles and most important, began to think about the way the organization traditionally went about replacing them. The planning staffs decided to look into the future and–based on the Coast Guard missions of maritime safety, maritime law enforcement, marine environmental protection and defense operations–find methods for meeting them in 2004 and beyond.

At the Coast Guard headquarters level, representatives from aviation, marine safety, marine engineering, operations, personnel and training all were included in crafting the Deepwater concept. Everyone would be represented in the process.

Instead of working the problem strictly within the Coast Guard, they elected to bring industry into the process. In effect, they told industry what the service must be capable of doing and asked, "based on your knowledge of technology, what is the best approach and the correct mix of assets to accomplish the mission?" In August, 1998, three teams of companies were awarded $7 million contracts to begin the concept development of the Deepwater Project. The intention was not to focus on individual acquisitions, but to build a system that was completely compatible from the beginning. Deepwater would represent an entirely new Coast Guard.

The industry teams were given only three constraints. The Coast Guard will always be a military organization, multi-missioned, and a maritime organization. Otherwise, all bets were off! Industry was given a clean sheet of paper and told to come up with a concept and a system.

Teams included Avondale Industries, working with Boeing-McDonnell Douglas Corporation and John J. McMullen Associates; Lockheed-Martin Government Electronic Systems working with Ingalls Shipbuilding; and Science Applications International Corporation working with Sikorsky Aircraft Corporation, Bath Ironworks and Marinette Marine.

An important component of the Deepwater Project will be the implementation of an extensive command, control, communications, computers, intelligence, sensors and reconnaissance system. The provision of these vital capabilities will allow the Coast Guard to locate, identify and classify targets. Today, such a capability is virtually nonexistent, especially when compared to those of the Navy. Considering that the Coast Guard comes under the command of the Navy in time of military action, such compatibility is critical.

The Deepwater Project will answer questions concerning how Coast Guard vessels are to be manned. Will maintenance sailors be aboard or will they stay at the home port in consolidated teams? Will sailors be trained to handle unmanned reconnaissance aircraft? Will vessels and aircraft be concentrated or spread out along the coasts?

Although the Coast Guard defined deepwater as beyond 50 miles, in truth the decisions made for the project will directly impact on the inshore units, since all the assets must be capable of interacting in a coherent manner. To this extent, the Keeper-Class tenders are an integral part of the Deepwater Project.

One of the biggest challenges to be overcome will be the acceptance of the Deepwater concept by the Coast Guard itself. People by nature are resistant to change and Deepwater is change.

Plans call for the award of the final Deepwater design and construction contract to be awarded to one of the three industry teams in 2002. In 10 years the Coast Guard could be an entirely different organization, one based on the information age and doing its mission with leading-edge technology.

Footnotes

1. A dracone is a special oil recovery storage bladder.

2. At this writing, problems are being experienced with the overall system which could result in its deletion.

Bibliographical Sources

Books:

Adamson, Hans Christian. *Keepers of the Lights*. New York: Greenberg Publisher, 1955.

Birse, Sheppard. *Lore of the Wreckers*. Boston: Beacon Press, 1961.

Brewerton, George D. Ida Lewis, *The Heroine of Lime Rock*. 1869.

Carter, Edwin Clarence. *The Territorial Papers of the United States, Volume XXIV, The Territory of Florida*. Washington, DC: National Archives, 1977.

Carter, *Territorial Papers*. Volume XXII.

Carter, *Territorial Papers*. Volume XXV.

Clifford, Mary Louise and Clifford, Candace. *Women Who Kept the Lights*. Williamsburg, VA: Cypress Communications, 1993.

Dean, Love. *Lighthouses of the Florida Coast*. Key West, Florida: Historic Florida Keys Foundation, 1992.

Dictionary of American Naval Fighting Ships, Volume III. Washington, DC: Naval History Division, 1967.

Floherty, John. *Sentinels of the Sea*. New York: J.B. Lippincott Company, 1955.

Gibbs, James A. *Sentinels of the North Pacific*. Portland, OR: Binfords and Mort, 1955.

Ludlum, David M. *Early American Hurricanes*. Boston: American Meteorological Society, 1967.

Mahon, John K. *History of the Second Seminole War, 1834-1842*. Gainsville, FL: The University of Florida Press, 1967.

Mason, Herbert Molloy. *Death From the Sea, Our Greatest Natural Disaster, the Galveston Hurricane of 1900*. New York: The Dial Press, 1967.

Noble, Dennis. *Lighthouses and Keepers*. Annapolis, MD: U.S. Naval Institute Press, 1997.

Ousley, Clarence. *Galveston in Nineteen Hundred*. Atlanta, GA: William C. Chase, 1900.

Putnam, George R. *Lighthouses and Lightships of the United States*. New York: Houghton-Mifflin, 1917.

Scheina, Robert L. *U.S. Coast Guard Cutters and Craft, 1946-90*. Annapolis, MD: U.S. Naval Institute Press, 1990.

Shanks, Ralph and Shanks, Lisa Woo. *Guardians of the Golden Gate, Lighthouses and Lifeboat Stations of San Francisco Bay*. Petaluma, CA: Costano Books, 1990.

Snow, Edward Rowe. *Famous New England Lighthouses*. Boston: Yankee Publishing, 1945.

Sterling, Robert Thayer. *Lighthouses of the Maine Coast and the Men Who Keep Them*. Battleboro, VT: Stephen Daye Press, 1935.

Viele, John. The Florida Keys, *A History of the Pioneers*. Sarasota, Florida: Pineapple Press, 1996.

Government Sources:

"Lighthouse Superintendent's Letter File." NARA, RG 26.

U.S. Coast Guard Naming Files, various files.

RG 26, NARA.

U.S. Department of Commerce, *Great Lakes Light List*, various years.

Internet:

Abbot, Elizabeth, "Ida Lewis," [http://www.projo.com/special/women/94root9.htm], January 20, 1999.

Bansemer, Roger. "Sand Key Lighthouse." [http:bansemer.cfnet.com/Fl-lighthouses/Sand%Key.htm]. February 1999.

"A Bit of History." [http://www1.shore.net/%7Egfisher/tia/history.htm], February 14, 1999.

"Bolivar Lighthouse." [http://www.crystalbeach.com/light.htm], February 12, 1999.

"Cape Elizabeth Light to Change." [http://www.lhdigest.com/archives/1998/sept98/Capeliz.htm]. February 12, 1999.

"Grace Darling Story," [http://www.bandol.u-net.com/grace.htm], August 15, 1999.

"Ida Lewis,"[http://www.providenceri.com/narragansettbay/ida_lewis.html], August 15, 1999.

"Idawally Zorada Lewis," [http://www.edgenet.net/redwood/notables/IDA_LEWIS.htm]. January 20, 1999.

Johns, Mary, "Abbie Burgess Launched," [http://www.lhdigest.com/archives/1887/may97/Burgess.htm], February 3, 1999.

"Key West Lighthouse." [http://bansemer.cftnet.com/Fl-lighthouse/Key%20West.htm], February 12, 1999.

"Medal of Honor Citations." [http://www.army.mil/cmh-pg/mohciv.htm].

"New Dungeness Lighthouse."[http://www.maine.com/lights/dungeness.htm], February 10, 1999.

"Scotch Cap Lighthouse," [http://www.usalights.com/alaska/scotchcap.htm], February 14, 1999.

"Scotch Cap Lighthouse Disaster," [http://www.teleport.com/~alany/uscg/ltsa.htm], February 14, 1999.

Interviews:

Grady Tate, October 13, 1999.

Suzanne Tale, August 12, 1999.

Journals:

Harrington, Frances. "The Heroine of Lime Rock," *Oceans*, 1985.

Harper's Weekly, July 31, 1869.

Mooney, Michael J. "Tidal Waves." *Alaska*, June 1976/

New England Historical and Genealogical Register, Volume 152, October 1998.

Putnam's Magazine. nd.

Taylor, Thomas W. "The First Key West Lighthouse." *Keepers Log*, Spring, 1995.

Ditto "The Second Key West Lighthouse." *Keepers Log*, Summer, 1995.

Rutherford, Don. "Disaster at Scotch Cap." *Keepers Log*, Winter, 1986.

West, Elizabeth. "Fifty Years at Lime Rock," *Cobblestone*, June 1981.

National Archives:

"Clipping File," Ida Lewis Light, NARA, RG 26.

"Clipping File," Sand Key, NARA, RG 26.

"Journal of the Light Station at Humbolt Bay Fog Signal." December 1916.

"Memorandum, Chief Radio Electrician Hoban B. Sanford, USCG."

Newspapers:

Boston Journal. June 20, 1870.

Galveston Daily News. August 30, 1915.

Miami Herald. November 14, 1989.

New York Times. March 5, 1906; October 22, 25, 26, 29, November 2, 1911.

New York Tribune. November 2, 1846.

Rockland Gazette (Rockland, ME). May 20, 1875.

Annuals:

Annual Report of the U.S. Life Saving Service, 1881, 1885. Government Printing Office.

Annual Report of the Commissioner of Lighthouses, various issues, Government Printing Office.

Coast Guard Bulletin, 1916, 1939.

Light List, Atlantic and Gulf Coasts of the United States, 1915. Washington, DC: Government Printing Office, 1915.

Lighthouse Service Bulletin, 1912; July, 1913; October 1915, January 1, February 1, September 1, November 1, 1916; February 1, April 2, May 1, 1917; February 1, 1933.

Unpublished Manuscript:

Pleger, Thomas C. *Green Island Light-Station, Wisconsin, A Synthesis of Related Historical and Archaeological Data*, 1992.

About The Author

Frederick Stonehouse holds a Master of Arts Degree in History from Northern Michigan University, Marquette Michigan, and has authored many books on Great Lakes maritime history. *Went Missing, Lake Superior's "Shipwreck Coast," Dangerous Coast: Pictured Rocks Shipwrecks, The Wreck of the Edmund Fitzgerald* and *Great Lakes Lighthouse Tales* are all published by Avery Color Studios, Inc.

He has also been a consultant for both the U.S. National Park Service and Parks Canada, and an "on air" expert for National Geographic Explorer and the History Channel as well as many regional media productions. He has also taught Great Lakes Maritime History at Northern Michigan University and is an active consultant for numerous Great Lakes oriented projects and programs. Currently he is teaching an on-line, web based course on Great Lakes Lighthouses at "Learninglighthouses.com."

His articles have been published in *Skin Diver, Great Lakes Cruiser Magazine* and *Lake Superior Magazine*. He is a member of the Board of Directors of the Marquette Maritime Museum and a member of the Board of Directors of the United States Life Saving Service Heritage Association.

Stonehouse resides in Marquette, Michigan.

Other Fred Stonehouse titles by Avery Color Studios, Inc.

- *Went Missing*
- *Lake Superior's Shipwreck Coast*
- *Dangerous Coast: Pictured Rock Shipwrecks*
- *Great Lakes Lighthouse Tales*
- *The Wreck of the Edmund Fitzgerald*